W9-AZL-253

TIME for KiDS

BIG BOOK OF HOW

TIME for KiDS

© 2017 Time Inc. Books

Published by Liberty Street, an imprint of Time Inc. Books
225 Liberty Street
New York, NY 10281

LIBERTY STREET and TIME For Kids are trademarks of Time Inc.

All rights reserved. No part of this book may be reproduced in any form or by any electronic or mechanical means, including information storage and retrieval systems, without permission in writing from the publisher, except by a reviewer, who may quote brief passages in a review.

SCOUT
BOOKS & MEDIA

Produced by Scout Books & Media Inc
President and Project Director Susan Knopf
Editor Margaret Parrish
Managing Editor Brittany Gialanella
Copyeditor Stephanie Engel
Proofreader Beth Adelman
Indexer ARC Indexing
Designer Dirk Kaufman

Writers
James Buckley, Jr. (Sports, Buildings, Home Technology, Space)
Michael Centore (Science, Computer Technology, Just for Fun)
Cari Jackson (Animals, Transportation, The Human Body, You and Your World)

Advisers
Special thanks to our expert reviewers, whose passion for and willingness to share their knowledge of their fields inspires us all: Elizabeth Bland; Amy Lennard Goehner; Paul McLean, PhD; Mary-Margaret Segraves, PhD, RN; Michael Rentz, PhD.

Thanks to the Time Inc. Books team: Margot Schupf, Anja Schmidt, Beth Sutinis, Deirdre Langeland, Georgia Morrissey, Hillary Leary, and Alex Voznesenskiy.

Special thanks to the TIME For Kids team: Nellie Cutler Gonzalez and Elizabeth Winchester.

ISBN: 978-1-68330-010-6
Library of Congress Control Number: 2017942484

Second Edition, 2017
1 QGT 17
10 9 8 7 6 5 4 3 2 1

We welcome your comments and suggestions about Time Inc. Books.

Please write to us at:
Time Inc. Books
Attention: Book Editors
P.O. Box 62310
Tampa, FL 33662-2310
(800) 765-6400

timeincbooks.com

Time Inc. Books products may be purchased for business or promotional use. For information on bulk purchases, please contact Christi Crowley in the Special Sales Department at (845) 895-9858.

A NOTE TO READERS AND THEIR PARENTS

An adult should supervise some of the activities in this book. They may require the use of scissors or other sharp objects, or need safety guidance from an adult. On the following pages, you will find a red star ⭐: pages 36–37, 104–105, 132–133, 148–149, and 180–181. When you reach a page that has a star, ask an adult for help.

HOW to use this book

This book has all the questions . . . and all the answers. If you've ever wondered how the dinosaurs died out, how an enormous cruise ship stays afloat, or how to perform the skateboard trick called an ollie, you'll find out in these pages. The book is divided into 11 chapters that cover topics ranging from sports and science to computers and animals. At the end of each chapter, you'll find hands-on activities. The book is also full of unusual facts that'll have you saying, "How about that!" A glossary at the end defines some of the terms used in the book.

Color guide Each chapter is color-coded, starting with the opening spread and seen in chapter headlines throughout.

Fast Fact and Did You Know? Read these to learn some amazing facts and trivia about the subject.

Introduction This will give you background information about the topic to help you understand both the question and the answer.

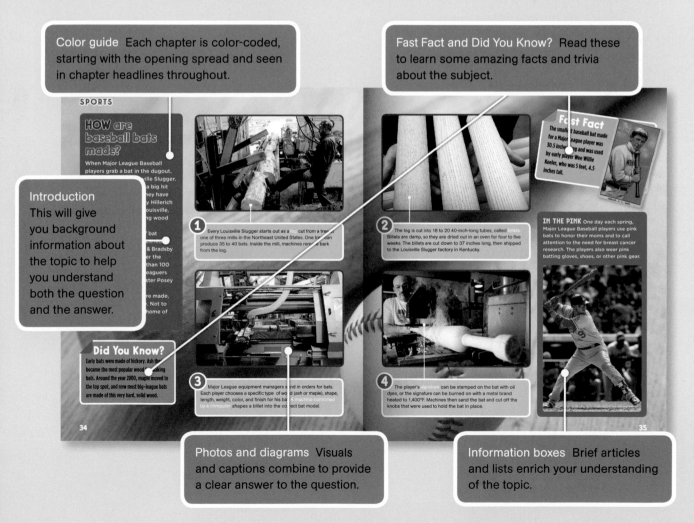

Photos and diagrams Visuals and captions combine to provide a clear answer to the question.

Information boxes Brief articles and lists enrich your understanding of the topic.

CHAPTER 1

ANIMALS

HOW did the dinosaurs die out?

The first dinosaurs appeared on Earth about 230 million years ago. Dinosaurs (the word means "terrible lizards") ruled the planet for nearly 165 million years. Then, about 66 million years ago, they all disappeared. Along with the dinos, at least 50% of all the planet's plants and animals were wiped out in a mass extinction. Extinction is the death of an entire species.

What caused this huge wipeout? Scientists have come up with several possibilities.

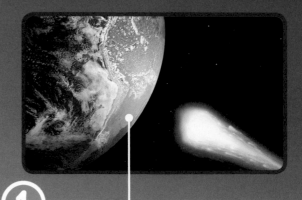

1 **THE BIG CRASH** A comet or asteroid about six miles across may have slammed into the shallow waters off the coast of southern Mexico 66 million years ago. The blast could have ignited a mineral called gypsum below the seafloor, which would have created a giant sulfur cloud that blocked the sun. A global winter would have resulted, killing off the dinos. Scientists now think that if the asteroid had hit just a few moments earlier or later, dinosaurs might still be alive today! Instead of landing in shallow waters, the asteroid would have hit the deep ocean— so no sulfur cloud, and a happy ending for the dinos.

2 **BLOWING THEIR TOPS** Before the dinosaurs died out, huge volcanic eruptions took place in western India. They covered half of modern-day India with a layer of volcanic rock one mile thick. Clouds of ash and dust could have blocked out the sun, lowering the planet's temperatures. Volcanic gases may have produced acid rain, which would have hurt plant and sea life. These disasters could have led to mass extinctions.

The first living things appeared on Earth about 3.5 billion years ago. Since then, animal species—from sponges to elephants—have developed fantastic features that help them survive.

Did You Know?

Among the animals that survived the extinction of the dinosaurs 65 million years ago were crocodiles and alligators. In fact, their body shapes haven't changed much since that time long ago.

Here today . . . Many scientists think a mass extinction may be going on right now. They estimate that 30,000 species disappear each year. That's three species an hour. By the end of this century, half of today's species of plants and animals could disappear. The main cause for this: humans.

A species is endangered when it is in immediate danger of becoming extinct. A threatened species is likely to become endangered in the future. Once a species is extinct, it will never come back. Here are just a handful of the thousands of animal species that are endangered or threatened.

Whooping crane   Jaguar

Black-footed ferret   Lowland gorilla

For more information on threatened species, go to *iucnredlist.org*.

4

SEA THIS Scientists believe that Earth's oceans were once much higher than they are today. Then, millions of years ago, the continents rose and sea levels dropped. Many once-wet areas became cool and dry. During that period, for example, North America was divided by a sea called the Interior Seaway. As the ocean levels lowered, the seaway drained. Many sea animals died, and the dry land could no longer produce the food that dinosaurs needed to survive. This may have caused them to die.

3

BAD BUGS As the planet's temperature rose 66 million years ago, it became a perfect breeding ground for germs and insects. The insects could have spread new diseases that dinosaurs and other animals couldn't fight off.

HOW do snakes move without legs?

Contrary to popular belief, snakes are not slimy. In fact, their scaly skin feels rough, which is the key to how they get around. The rectangular ventral (belly) scales on a snake's underside work like the treads on a tire, gripping the ground. A snake has segmented muscles, which allow body parts to move separately and make it possible for the snake to change the angle of its scales to the ground—the steeper the angle, the stronger the grip. The scales act like hooks that pull the snake forward. Snakes can even grasp smooth surfaces and fine grains of sand.

Neck vertebrae do not have ribs. They attach the head to the body.

FLEXIBLE BACKBONE

The backbone is a column of up to 585 vertebrae, bones that protect the spinal cord. Longer snake species often have more vertebrae than shorter species.

Each vertebra has a pair of ribs attached to it.

Strong, flexible spine allows the snake to move in different ways.

WAYS SNAKES MOVE
Their many vertebrae and ribs give snakes the ability to get around in different ways. They can move through water, across hot surfaces, up trees, and around rocky areas.

SIDEWINDING The aptly named sidewinder rattlesnake lifts its head and throws itself forward, with its body following. Only two points of the snake's body touch the ground at any one time. Two waves move down the snake's body during this movement—one up and down, and one side to side. The sidewinder rattlesnake can travel up to 18 miles per hour through fine sand.

LATERAL UNDULATION (OR SERPENTINE LOCOMOTION) The snake moves its head from side to side. This begins a wavelike series of S curves that move down the body through muscle contractions. The snake pushes against water or resistance points on land to move forward. Serpentine locomotion doesn't work very well on smooth surfaces. The snakes that use this type of motion use it when they are on land or in water.

CONCERTINA LOCOMOTION The snake bends the lower part of its body to grip a tree or brace against the sides of a tunnel. It stretches out the front part of its body, then comes to rest. Finally, it scrunches the rest of its body like an accordion. Snakes use the concertina method of locomotion for climbing and burrowing.

RECTILINEAR (OR CATERPILLAR) LOCOMOTION A heavy snake, such as a python or a boa, moves in much the same way as a caterpillar. The snake engages two types of muscles to lift up and push off the ground, using the friction (the rubbing together of two objects) of its belly scales to move itself forward. The S shape curves up and down, rather than side to side, in a rippling effect.

HOW do sharks find prey?

Sharks are swift and silent hunters. They have keen senses that help them focus in on prey—from an extra-sharp sense of smell to receptors that enable them to sense the movement of other animals in the water.

Many large sharks, such as great whites, have big appetites. They will track down and eat seals, sea lions, and other marine animals. Some will even swallow garbage floating around in the ocean, such as license plates and metal cans. Although most sharks don't like people on their menu, some do bite humans.

Sharks have been swimming in Earth's oceans for more than 400 million years. One ancient shark was 52 feet long and had teeth the size of a person's hand. Today's sharks are smaller, but they remain at the top of the food chain in the ocean. A close look at their bodies shows why they are such hardy survivors. From nose to tail, they're packed with sensory equipment that helps them locate their prey.

NOSE A shark can smell even a tiny drop of blood in the water from hundreds of yards away. It can detect a single drop of blood in 1 million drops of water. That's like smelling a teaspoon of juice in a swimming pool.

EXTRA SENSE Small openings in the shark's skin called electroreceptors detect tiny electrical fields created by the heartbeat and muscle movements of other fish. This lets the shark hunt for prey that might be hiding under the sand.

EYES A shark can see in dim light because its eyes are about 10 times more sensitive to light than human eyes are. Some sharks have membranes that cover and protect their eyes when they attack prey.

Did You Know?

Sharks are hungry even before they are born. A shark develops teeth while it is still inside its mother. Sometimes one unborn shark will eat its unborn brothers and sisters.

EARS Tiny holes on top of the head give a shark very sensitive ears. It can pick up the sound of a struggling fish more than 800 feet away.

MOTION A row of vibration-sensitive hair cells runs along the shark's sides. They allow the shark to sense the faintest motion of a fish from about three to 10 feet away.

TFK SPECIAL REPORT

SHARK BITE! Sharks prefer eating other marine animals to eating people. Still, the number of shark attacks has been up in recent years. Researchers think one reason is that there are more people swimming, boogie boarding, and surfing than ever before. Volusia County, Florida, holds the U.S. record for shark attacks. It has a long coastline and its beaches are packed with swimmers. A shark may think a human foot is a flounder, then spit it out after the first bite.

Humans are, in fact, a bigger threat to sharks than sharks are to people. One hundred million sharks are killed each year through hunting or as bycatch.

Fast Fact

Humans add fluoride to toothpaste to coat their teeth with fluorapatite, a hard mineral that protects teeth from cavities. Shark teeth are covered in it naturally. Most sharks can also replace their teeth constantly—some use up to 30,000 teeth in a lifetime!

HOW do chameleons change color?

Chameleons can change their colors in seconds, from brown to green to red to blue. Experts believe light, temperature, and mood affect the lizard's color. A chameleon might turn to green to reflect sunlight and stay cool. Or it might become darker to absorb the sun's heat. An angry chameleon can turn red or yellow to warn other chameleons to back off.

The secret to this color explosion is skin deep. Under a chameleon's skin is a layer made up of red or yellow pigment (color) cells. Another layer contains crystals called guanine. Other cells have particles called melanin, which can make colors darker.

Nerves direct pigment cells to tighten or relax or cause melanin to spread throughout other layers. If a chameleon is angry, the cells with guanine spread apart and change the color reflected from blue to red or yellow. Pigments also blend to produce different colors. When a chameleon is relaxed, the guanine cells reflect blue, which combines with the yellow pigment to look green.

The skin is green or brown when the chameleon is resting. This helps it blend into the background. Pigments under the skin change the lizard's color, depending on temperature, sunlight, and mood.

The body is narrow and shaped like a leaf, making it easy to blend in on trees, where chameleons hang out.

The prehensile tail can curl and wrap around branches.

Fast Fact

Chameleons are found in Africa, southern Europe, and Asia. There are more than 80 different types. The largest are nearly two feet long.

To change color, a chameleon makes its color cells larger or smaller. It can also make its skin darker by letting a chemical called melanin rise to the upper cell layers.

The eyes move independently of one another, so each eye can look at different objects at the same time.

The fingers and toes are able to grip branches.

Red and yellow color cells

Melanin layer

Guanine cells

COLOR GUARD

Here are some other animals that protect themselves by changing colors.

As it swims along the bottom of the sea, the flounder can change its color and patterns in seconds to blend in with the ocean floor. It can make itself look like almost anything, from sand to pebbles. A young flounder is transparent, so no predator can see it. It changes color as it matures.

The satanic leaf-tailed gecko is incredibly hard to spot. Not only does its color pattern blend in with the foliage where it lives, but its leaf-shaped tail also looks decayed at the edges, and it has a flap of skin along its body that keeps it from casting a shadow.

This arachnid hangs out on either white or yellow flowers, waiting for a tasty meal to come along. If the goldenrod crab spider is on a yellow flower, it squeezes a liquid yellow pigment into its outer cell layer. If it sits on a white flower, it gets rid of the yellow liquid so only white cells show.

HOW do squid light up?

Bioluminescence is a chemical reaction that occurs in many types of marine animals, including squid, worms, fish, bacteria, plankton, and even sharks. Squid (and other cephalopods) light up thanks to a chemical reaction called bioluminescence. Photophores in their skin contain the substances luciferin and luciferase, which together cause a chemical reaction. Some animals produce their own luciferin. Others, like squid, absorb it through food.

Although glowing marine animals put on quite a show, they don't light up just for entertainment. Bioluminescent squid use their shimmering displays to communicate, find mates, lure prey, or keep themselves from becoming prey.

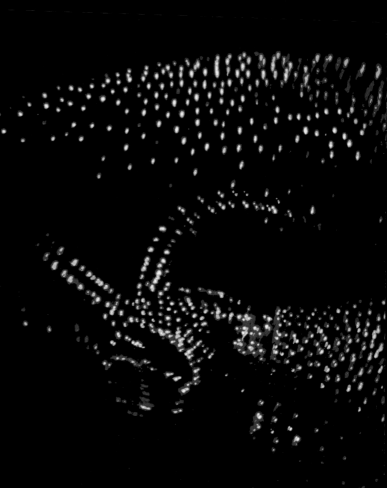

OTHER FLASHY SEA CREATURES

A few nights after a full moon, female Bermuda fireworms swim to the surface from the ocean floor and start a wild dance party. They glow and swirl in circles to attract mates. Males join them, flashing their lights back at the females.

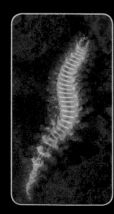

Fireworm

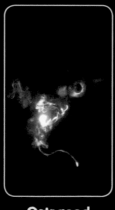

Ostracod

The ostracod (a small crustacean) spits glowing mucus when threatened or grabbed. The bright goo lights up the attacker and frightens it. The light might also attract bigger predators that could eat the attacker, so it spits out the ostracod.

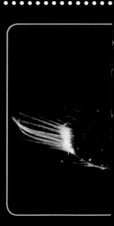

Every year, firefly squid migrate from deep to shallow waters off the coast of Japan to breed. People gather to watch the light show.

HOW DO OCEAN WAVES LIGHT UP?

In Southern California, red tides happen often in the summer. The thick bloom of red algae attracts single-celled plankton that light up when agitated. When waves crash through the sea of plankton, the water turns a brilliant turquoise.

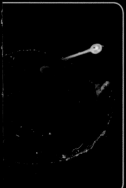

An anglerfish can't light up by itself. Instead, it is home to bioluminescent bacteria that live in a small organ called an esca. The esca dangles off the anglerfish's head like a fishing rod, luring prey straight into the danger zone.

Anglerfish

Black dragonfish

Light waves travel in different wavelengths, which determine the color of the light. Red light has long wavelengths and doesn't reach the deep sea. This is why many deep-sea creatures are red—it's like being invisible. Black dragonfish are able to emit and see red light. They can spot red prey and also communicate with other dragonfish without being detected. Sneaky!

HOW do animals see at night?

For most people, night is the time to catch some z's. But many animals start their day at sundown. Animals that sleep during the day and are active at night are nocturnal. For them, nighttime is the right time.

For nocturnal critters, finding food in the dark depends on great eyesight. Their eyes are specially adapted to let them see in dim light. Human eyes take a while to adjust in low light. Even then, we can see only shades of black and white, and not much detail. That's why we keep stubbing our toes at night! But nocturnal animals adjust instantly. The vision of some animals is so sharp, they can detect forms in almost total darkness.

The giant peepers of the tarsier, a tiny primate from Southeast Asia, let in extra light to help it see at night.

THE NOCTURNAL EYE

The pupils open wider than those of humans at night, allowing nocturnal animals to take in more light.

Pupil

Iris

Lens

Retina (Rods & Cones)

Tapetum

A nocturnal animal doesn't have many cones, or color-sensitive cells, in its retina. Instead, the retina is packed with rods, which are cells that detect light, not color. These cells work in dim light and can sense motion.

Some animals with eyeballs that can't move have rounded lenses. Rounded lenses let an animal focus light coming in from any angle.

The tapetum (tah-pee-tum) is a thin membrane behind the retina, which contains cells sensitive to light. When light passes through the retina, the tapetum reflects it back like a mirror. This gives the retina a double dose of light, making it easier to see in darkness.

IN THE DARK Animals have all kinds of special adaptations that let them hunt—and avoid hunters—in dim light and even in total darkness.

OWL An owl has great night vision thanks to a very wide retina, an iris that opens up to twice the width of a hawk's, and a lens that works like a telescope. It can focus on a mouse more than the length of a football field away on a dark night.

COLOSSAL SQUID Even considering its 40-foot-long body, the colossal squid has enormous eyes. These basketball-sized eyes—the biggest in the animal kingdom—help the squid detect a major predator, the sperm whale, in the darkness thousands of feet below the ocean's surface.

BAT A bat sends out a high-pitched sound that bounces off objects, including tasty insects. The bat uses the echoes to "see" what's around it.

SPOOKFISH The spookfish looks like it has four eyes, but in reality it has only two. Each eye is divided into two parts by tissue lined with crystals, which act as a mirror to reflect and focus light in the eye. This helps the spookfish make the most of what little light there is in the deep sea.

HOW does a spider spin its web?

Itsy-bitsy spiders—and some that aren't so itsy-bitsy—live everywhere on Earth, except for the polar regions. They crawl around in dry deserts, on mountains, underground, in oceans—and possibly in some corners of your home.

Most spiders are web masters. A gland in a spider's abdomen produces silk. The silk is pushed through a body part called a spinneret and comes out as a thread. Some spiders spin silk webs that look like big white sheets. Some webs look like tiny drops stretched across plants or grass. One of the most common webs is the orb web, which is shown in the photo. This is the kind you see on Halloween or in spooky haunted houses in scary movies. A spider waits at the center of the orb web for a tasty insect to land. This makes the web vibrate. The spider knows from the vibration whether or not the visitor is food. If the spider is lucky, dinner is served!

MAKING AN ORB WEB

1 The spider finds a good spot, such as a tree branch, and makes a strand of silk. The dangling strand sticks to another branch. The spider attaches the other end of the strand to the branch it's standing on. Then it crosses back and forth over that strand, strengthening it with more strands.

2 The spider makes a loose strand connecting the two ends of the first strand. Next, it drops down a strand at the middle of the loop to form a Y shape. These three strands are the first spokes of the web.

3 The spider spins a frame around the Y-shaped spokes. The rest of the spokes will be attached to the frame.

A REAL SPIDER-MAN Steven Kutcher knows spiders. He is an entomologist, a scientist who studies insects. People in Hollywood call him a bug wrangler. For more than 20 years, Kutcher has been rounding up bugs and helping them get roles in movies and TV. He worked on the first three Spider-Man movies, as well as many others in which insects played a supporting role.

During "auditions," Kutcher doesn't look for insects that can act. He looks for bugs that can get the job done. For *Spider-Man*, for instance, Kutcher studied what the spider would have to do—spin a web, for example, or climb a wall. Then he determined which type of spider would perform the task best.

Kutcher hopes that insect-filled movies will help turn bug-fearing folks into fans.

The spider's silk comes out of the spinneret.

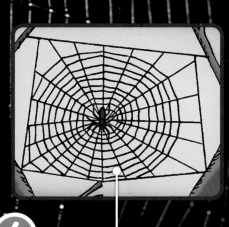

4 The spider makes more spokes. Each spoke is close enough that the spider can walk on one while making another. Spokes also must be close enough that the spider can walk across them when the web is complete. These threads are not sticky.

5 When the spokes are finished, the spider creates a few circular threads in the center of the web to make it strong. Then it spins a spiral of non-sticky thread from the center of the web to the edge of the frame. This helps the spider construct the rest of the web.

6 The spider spins many more spiral strands using sticky threads. When finished, the spider removes the non-sticky spiral. Total time for building the web: about 30 minutes. Some spiders build a new web every day, while others just repair any damage.

HOW do sea otters stay warm?

With their fuzzy ears and round black eyes, sea otters might be the cutest of all marine mammals. They live in shallow coastal waters in the northern Pacific Ocean—that is some cold water! And yet you won't see sea otters shivering.

Unlike most marine mammals, this member of the weasel family doesn't have blubber to keep it warm. Instead, an otter relies on the densest fur in the animal kingdom. Its fur can have up to 1 million superfine hairs per square inch. The fur traps a layer of air against the otter's body, and its body heat warms this layer of air. This insulates the otter from the cold water.

BY THE NUMBERS This amazing fur once made sea otters targets of hunters. In the early 1900s, fewer than 2,000 sea otters remained worldwide. Today, there are more than 106,000 sea otters, although they continue to be an endangered species. They live along the coastlines of Alaska, Russia, California, and Mexico.

RAFTERS Sea otters spend most of their time floating on their backs. They often float in large groups called rafts, with males in separate groups from females and pups. The rafts can have just a few sea otters, or hundreds—especially in Alaska, where the otter population is greatest. Otters hold hands to stay together. They also wrap themselves in kelp to keep from floating away.

BATH TIME Dirty fur doesn't provide good insulation, which is why sea otters spend more time grooming themselves than any other animal. For two to three hours a day, they rub, roll, and blow air into their fur. Oil spills caused by offshore drilling threaten sea otter populations—the oil mats otters' fur, making it impossible for them to stay warm.

TABLE FOR ONE Sea otters also stay warm by eating—a lot. They eat up to 30% of their body weight per day, dining on invertebrates such as sea urchins, mussels, and crabs. They can dive 250 feet down to the seafloor, then tuck their prey in their armpits as they swim back to the surface. Sea otters float on their backs and use their bellies as tables. They use rocks as tools to crack open shells.

WHY ARE SEA OTTERS IMPORTANT FOR ECOSYSTEMS? Sea otters help combat climate change. They are a keystone species, which means that their behavior affects many other animals. Sea urchins, tasty treats for otters, feast on kelp. Otters eat large numbers of sea urchins, which means kelp forests grow bigger if otters are there to keep urchin numbers in check. Kelp forests absorb carbon dioxide, protecting the atmosphere from global warming. When sea otters are around, kelp forests are able to absorb 12 times more carbon dioxide than when otters aren't present.

Sea otters also help protect coastlines from agricultural runoff by eating crabs. Farm pollution causes algae to grow on sea grass, eventually destroying the grass. Crabs feed on the animals that eat the algae. By eating more crabs, the otters allow these algae-eating organisms to thrive, keeping the sea grass healthy. Many species of fish use the grasses as nurseries for their eggs and offspring.

HOW do hummingbirds hover?

While some birds can use the wind to stay fixed in one place in the air, hummingbirds are the only birds that truly hover. They are also the only birds able to fly backward. To accomplish these feats, they require a great deal of power relative to their size.

The flight muscles that attach to the breastbone make up 25% to 30% of a hummingbird's body weight. The bird has flexible shoulder joints, with wings that are rigid from shoulder to tip. This allows the wings to move in a horizontal figure-eight pattern. The wings change the direction of thrust on the upstroke and downstroke, keeping the bird in place. A bird usually gets power only on the downstroke of its wings, but a hummingbird gets a quarter of its power from the upstroke.

A hummingbird moves its wings—and everything else—incredibly fast. The giant hummingbird beats its wings 10 to 15 times per second, while the amethyst woodstar, a much smaller hummingbird species, makes 80 wing beats per second. A hummingbird's heart rate reaches as high as 1,260 beats per minute. Even at rest, a hummingbird takes 250 breaths per minute.

All this activity requires a lot of fuel. Hummingbirds have the fastest metabolic rate of any vertebrate on Earth. They consume up to eight times their body weight in sugar every day, in addition to the insects they eat.

RAPID HOVER CYCLE

FLIGHT PATTERNS

Hummingbirds can fly forward, backward, sideways—even upside down!

WING MOVEMENT

HOVERING To hover, the hummingbird flaps its wings back and forth as it tilts its body slightly upward.

FORWARD The body is straight and the wings flap up and down for forward flight.

BACKWARD To fly backward, the bird flaps its wings above its head and holds its body upright.

HOW DO MALE HUMMINGBIRDS FIND MATES?

The Anna's hummingbird is a hummingbird species. The males perform jaw-dropping aerial acrobatics during courtship. They dive at speeds of 50 miles per hour, then stop abruptly just before they hit the ground. Relative to body size, that is the fastest dive in the animal kingdom. Consider this: Peregrine falcons dive at 200 body lengths per second, but the Anna's hummingbird dives at 383 body lengths per second. An astronaut would black out if he or she dove that quickly.

RESTING

When hummingbirds sleep, they enter a state called torpor, which allows them to conserve energy. They slow their heart rates to as low as 50 beats per minute, and sometimes they briefly hang upside down.

TAIL TALE

The male Anna's hummingbird sings with his tail. Wind blowing through the feathers creates a chirping noise. This display tells the female that he is a healthy bird, worthy of sharing his genes.

HOW do blue whales communicate?

Blue whales are the largest animals on Earth—and also the loudest! Like all whale species, blue whales use sound for many purposes: to navigate, detect food, and find a mate. Sound travels four times faster through water than through air, making it the most effective way for some whales to communicate. And the blue whale's deep groans, hums, grunts, and clicks are so loud they can travel thousands of miles through the ocean.

Blue whales are solitary animals and often travel alone. Even a calf and its mother might travel a mile apart, making long-distance communication vital. But scientists worry that noises from shipping, military sonar activity, and leisure boats are affecting how whales behave. Human sounds also may confuse whales. Noise pollution may also have decreased the distance that whales can communicate, from 1,000 miles in 1940 to just 100 miles today. If noise pollution prevents whales from locating mates, researchers worry it could be difficult to increase the population of this endangered species.

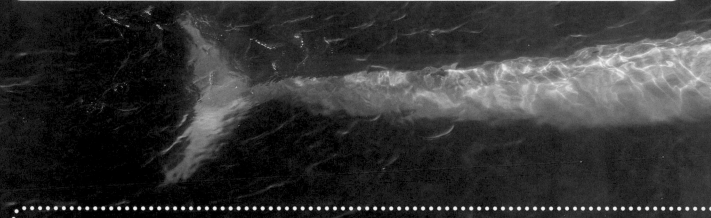

HOW ELEPHANTS COMMUNICATE

Body language When threatened, an elephant will raise its head and expand its ears to look even bigger. Its message: I'm ready to fight. It pulls back its ears when it wants to communicate that it's backing down.

CLICKS A whale uses clicks to navigate. The sound waves bounce off objects and return to the whale, enabling the whale to identify the objects. Clicks might also communicate messages to other whales.

WHISTLES AND PULSES Whistles and pulsed calls sound like squeaks and screams to humans. Whales use these sounds to socialize. Researchers have identified nine dialects, or distinctly different vocabularies of sound, used by whales in different parts of the sea.

TAILS AND FINS Whales make loud slapping noises on the water's surface that can be heard hundreds of feet below. These serve as warnings to other whales, or scare schools of fish together for easy meals.

Sounds An elephant can produce many sounds, from soft groans to screams. Each call has a meaning. Elephants know the individual sounds of hundreds of other elephants. Low-frequency calls travel as far as five miles. These growls help elephants communicate with herds miles away.

Trunk An elephant uses its trunk to smell odors produced by other elephants. These scents send messages about an elephant's health and emotions. As a way of saying hello, elephants of different groups will touch each other with their trunks as they pass. Males and females entwine their trunks when they're thinking about mating.

HOW does a caterpillar become a butterfly?

Does it take magic to turn a tubelike, hairy caterpillar into a graceful, shimmery butterfly? No—the caterpillar just needs to follow a life cycle called metamorphosis (meh-tih-*more*-fuh-siss), a word that means "changing shape."

Most insects go through a four-stage process called complete metamorphosis: egg → larva → pupa or chrysalis → adult. Others go through a three-stage process called simple metamorphosis: egg → nymph → adult.

Monarch butterflies go through complete metamorphosis. First, an egg hatches into a larva, called a caterpillar. Its job is to eat and grow. After about two weeks, it forms a chrysalis. Inside the chrysalis, the larva begins its complete change. The caterpillar has jaws for chewing, 12 eyes with poor vision, and legs for crawling. The butterfly will have sucking mouthparts to slurp nectar, two compound eyes with excellent vision, and wings that help it fly.

Butterfly egg

1 A female adult monarch butterfly lays her egg on a plant that will be food for the larva when it hatches. She secures the egg, which is a creamy white color, to a leaf with a sticky substance. After a few days, a tiny caterpillar hatches.

2 The little caterpillar eats constantly. When it grows too big for its skin, it sheds, revealing a new skin underneath. The caterpillar keeps eating, growing, and shedding until it has stored enough food for the transformation to come.

3 The fully grown caterpillar finds a safe place to attach itself. It spins a silky protective layer and wraps it around its body. This layer, with the insect inside, is called a chrysalis. Inside the chrysalis, the larva absorbs its own body. Some cells survive, and they divide to form the butterfly.

SIMPLE METAMORPHOSIS

Some insects go through a three-stage cycle called simple metamorphosis. They start out as eggs. When they hatch, the nymphs look like small versions of the adults. During the nymph stage, they shed their skins, or molt. The number of molts varies by insect species. Grasshoppers molt five times on the way to becoming adults.

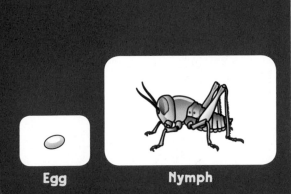

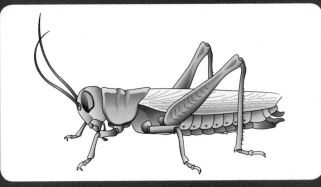

Egg   **Nymph**   **Adult**

As the third stage continues, wings, antennae, and a three-part body form. The chrysalis becomes transparent, showing wings covered in colored scales. The new butterfly pushes against the chrysalis and cracks it open.

4 The legs and antennae come out first, then the emerging butterfly uses its legs to pull the rest of its body out. It unfolds its wings and lets them dry before flying off to find food.

HOW DO BUTTERFLY WINGS FORM? As it grows, a caterpillar develops bumps on its body. Inside the chrysalis, the bumps become wings that are wet, folded, and squished into the small space. They stay that way when the butterfly emerges. After a few minutes, the butterfly uses its muscles to pump blood to the wings. The wings unfold and dry off. Then the butterfly is ready for its first flight.

HOW do orangutans build their homes?

In the Indonesian language, orangutan means "person of the forest." Found only on the Southeast Asian islands of Borneo and Sumatra, orangutans are the largest arboreal (tree-dwelling) mammals in the world. They spend almost all their lives in the treetops and build their homes there.

Adult orangutans build new nests daily. They choose horizontal branches and bend young, green branches inward to form structures like hammocks. They weave in sticks and line their nests with leafy branches. Large leaves serve as cover from the rain. Orangutans are born knowing how to build nests, but young orangutans watch others to become better builders.

NESTING A female orangutan carries her baby for the first two or three years. They use the nest for daytime naps, playtime, and sleeping.

LIFE IN TREES
Orangutans have skills and behaviors that are perfectly suited to life in the trees. Orangutans are not particularly social and tend to stay within a home range.

HANDS ON With opposable thumbs on both their hands and feet, orangutans can grasp and manipulate objects in the same way humans do. They also use their long, muscular arms and gripping hands and feet to swing through the treetops.

TASTY TREATS Orangutans spend 60% of their day foraging (searching) for food. Their diet includes leaves, bark, flowers, eggs, and, most importantly, more than 300 kinds of fruit. Orangutans can remember the location of every fruit-bearing tree in their forest, and even when each one ripens. For water, they chew moist leaves and drink water pooled on leaves.

BRINGING UP BABY Orangutan babies stay with their mothers for eight years, which is the longest childhood of any animal besides humans. Mothers teach their offspring how to move about the forest and how to find food. Young orangutans learn how to use leaves to handle prickly fruit and dig for seeds and insects with sticks. Once they are weaned (no longer drinking their mother's milk), orangutans live mostly solitary lives.

MALE CALL Adult male orangutans weigh around 200 pounds. Males have wide cheeks and large throat sacs. They communicate through long calls, each of which can last for a full minute. The calls attract mates and warn other males to stay away.

HOW TO care for a pet

Pets are a big responsibility. They require food, water, shelter, exercise, and medical care. A family needs to have the time, money, and space to create a happy home for an animal. Different kinds of pets have different needs. Here is how to care for a new dog.

What to do:

1 The first step to caring for your pet is choosing one that's right for you. Low-maintenance animals include fish, snakes, and reptiles. High-maintenance animals like dogs, birds, cats, and horses require a greater commitment in terms of time, care, and money. Discuss this as a family.

CAT CARE Cats may seem self-sufficient, but they still need good guardians. Here are just some of the things good cat owners should do for their pets:

* Just like humans, cats need good medical care. Your cat should have regular vet checkups and be vaccinated against dangerous diseases.
* Cats require the right food to stay healthy and active. Ask your vet to recommend a diet for your pet.
* Brush and comb your cat regularly.
* A happy cat has a clean, warm, dry place to sleep and rest.
* Clean the litter box daily.
* Provide your cat with a scratching post—a cat needs to groom its claws.

4 Obedience classes can be a good experience for both a puppy (or an adult dog) and its family. A class gives you and your dog a chance to learn about each other. A set schedule and consistent rules work best. A dog can become confused and upset if the rules are constantly changing.

2 If you've decided a dog is right for you, set aside a separate room or quiet space for your new pet to stay in when it arrives. Introduce the newcomer to other areas of the home gradually. If you have other pets, talk to a veterinarian about how to introduce a new pet into the home.

3 Bring your dog to the veterinarian for vaccinations and medical care. A veterinarian will also give you tips on how much and what type of food to feed your dog.

5 Make sure to provide adequate exercise. Dogs need several walks a day. Give your dog plenty of fresh water daily to keep it hydrated.

6 Set aside time every day to play with and groom your dog. Take time to know your pooch and make sure it feels comfortable with you. Be mindful of its need for quiet and space. Once it has given you the go-ahead, feel free to lavish it with lots of hugs and kisses.

CHAPTER 2

SPORTS

HOW does a soccer referee make a call?

On a huge soccer field with 22 players on two teams, the 23rd person on the field is the referee. It's his or her job to keep the game fair and safe by making sure players follow the rules. The key to the job is being in the right place at the right time. A referee works across the field in a diagonal line. By following that line as the ball moves up and down the field, the referee can see just about anything that happens. Plus, assistant referees are there to help out. When a player commits a foul, the referee blows a whistle and stops play.

1 There are 17 "laws," or rules, in soccer. Most fouls occur when one player pushes, trips, or knocks over the player who has the ball. If a player other than the goalie uses his hands or arms, that is a foul, too.

2 A ref shows a yellow card to a player who commits a foul. If the player makes a second serious foul, another yellow card is given. Two yellow cards result in an automatic red card. Once the red card is given, the player must leave the game and cannot be replaced. A violent or deliberate foul can result in a "straight red card."

3 A referee is part of a team, too. Two assistant referees, or linesmen, each cover half the field, running along the sidelines. Their job is to signal offside and the directions of throw-ins, goal kicks, or corner kicks. They also let the referee know when they spot fouls.

Top athletes need to keep current with the latest technologies, have the best equipment for their sport, and know all the right moves. But you don't need to be a pro to learn some awesome sports skills.

Did You Know?

In most sports, an official has to call every foul as it happens. A soccer referee doesn't. If a player is fouled but keeps possession of the ball or passes it to a teammate, the referee can signal "advantage" and instruct the teams to "play on." The reason? To prevent one team from fouling deliberately to slow down the other team.

4 The referee signals what type of kick will restart play after a foul.

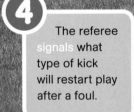

DIRECT KICK Arm pointed forward at an angle; the kicker can hit the ball directly into the goal.

INDIRECT KICK Arm raised straight up; two players need to touch the ball before it can go in the goal.

PENALTY KICK Arm pointed at penalty spot; the player gets to kick against the goalie alone from a spot 12 yards from the goal.

HOW are baseball bats made?

When Major League Baseball players grab a bat in the dugout, very often it's a Louisville Slugger. Louisville Sluggers are a big hit with ballplayers—and they have been since the company Hillerich & Bradsby, located in Louisville, Kentucky, began making wooden bats in 1884.

There are dozens of bat companies in the U.S., Canada, and Japan, but Hillerich & Bradsby is the most famous. Over the years, it has sold more than 100 million bats. Many big leaguers use them, including Buster Posey and Nelson Cruz.

To learn how bats are made, you have to head home. Not to home plate, but to the home of the Louisville Slugger.

Did You Know?

Early bats were made of hickory. Ash then became the most popular wood for making bats. Around the year 2000, maple moved to the top spot, and now most big-league bats are made of this very hard, solid wood.

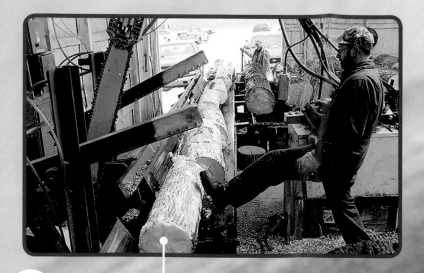

1 Every Louisville Slugger starts out as a log cut from a tree at one of three mills in the Northeastern United States. One tree can produce 35 to 40 bats. Inside the mill, machines remove bark from the log.

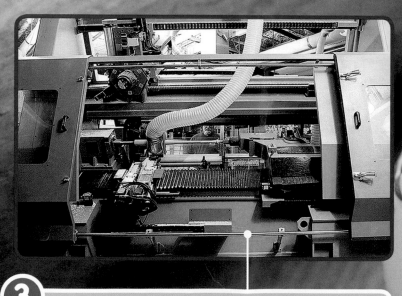

3 Major League equipment managers send in orders for bats. Each player chooses a specific type of wood (ash or maple), shape, length, weight, color, and finish for his bat. A machine controlled by a computer shapes a billet into the correct bat model.

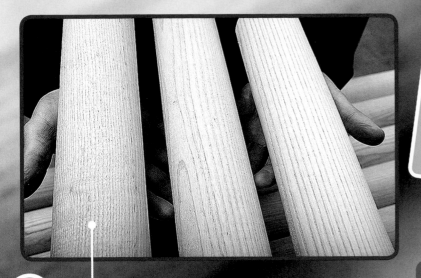

Fast Fact

The smallest baseball bat made for a Major League player was 30½ inches long and was used by early player Wee Willie Keeler, who was 5 feet, 4½ inches tall.

KEELER, N. Y. AMER.

② The log is cut into 18 to 20 40-inch-long tubes, called billets. Billets are damp, so they are dried out in an oven for four to five weeks. The billets are cut down to 37 inches long, then shipped to the Louisville Slugger factory in Kentucky.

IN THE PINK One day each spring, Major League Baseball players use pink bats to honor their moms and to call attention to the need for breast cancer research. The players also wear pink batting gloves, shoes, and other pink gear.

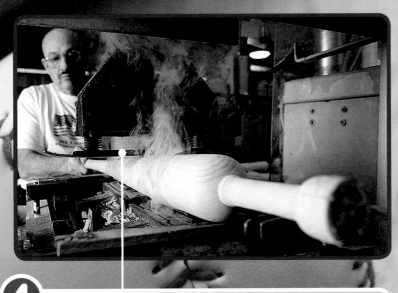

④ The player's signature can be stamped on the bat with oil dyes, or the signature can be burned on with a metal brand heated to 1,400°F. Machines then sand the bat and cut off the knobs that were used to hold the bat in place.

35

HOW do you do an ollie?

Remember to ask an adult for help.

In the 1950s, California surfers needed something fun to ride when there were no waves. So they invented the skateboard. The first skateboards looked more like scooters than like today's models. They were made of metal roller-skate wheels attached to a wooden board or box.

Skateboarding didn't really take off as a sport until 1973. In that year, plastic wheels were first attached to skateboards. Thanks to plastic wheels, a skater could go faster and do cool tricks, such as skating on two wheels (wheelies), spinning on the back wheels (pivot), or jumping over a bar and landing back on the board (hippie jump).

In 1976, a skater from Florida named Alan "Ollie" Gelfand invented a trick that let the skater pop the skateboard into the air. Gelfand's invention opened the way for many midair tricks. His trick is the one most beginning skateboarders learn first: the ollie.

Fast Fact

Tony Hawk is the king of skateboarders. He won 73 skateboarding contests, invented many tricks, and was the first skater to land a 900: two and a half spins in midair while on a board. He was inducted into the Skateboarding Hall of Fame in 2009.

TFK SPECIAL REPORT

Q&A WITH TONY HAWK

Many consider **Tony Hawk** the greatest skateboarder of all time. TIME FOR KIDS asked him some questions.

TFK: What did you feel when you started out as a young skater?
Hawk: When I first went to the skate park and I saw what was really possible—these guys were flying out of empty swimming pools—I was like, "I want to do that. I want to fly." So then I started going to skate parks on a regular basis. Every time I went, I would learn something new.

TFK: What advice do you have for beginning skaters?
Hawk: Take it slow. It takes repeated attempts to learn a kick flip and to develop skills. And you've got to work at it.

TFK: What advice do you have for kids who hope to achieve success?
Hawk: Do what you love doing, even if it doesn't seem like it's the coolest thing at the time. If you enjoy it, you have to follow it, because ultimately you're going to be happy going to work every day.

1 Put your front foot near the middle of the board, about two inches from where the bolt is. Your back foot should be on the tail, or back, of the board.

2 Bend both your legs and squat down. You should be ready to jump.

3 Slide the side of your front foot to the front of the board. At the same time, push down hard on the tail with your back foot. Your back leg should straighten as the tail hits the ground.

4 When the board is in the air, stop moving your front foot. Pull your knees up toward your chest. Raise your back foot so the board can rise until it is fairly level in the air.

5 When the board is level in the air and it begins to drop, straighten your legs.

6 As you land, bend your legs to absorb the shock. The board should be level as it lands, so all the wheels touch the ground at the same time. Both feet should be over the bolts. Your back foot should not be over the tail. Don't try this on a moving skateboard until you have mastered the trick.

HOW does a golfer choose the right club?

A golfer chooses each club based on the types of shots he or she has to hit. Different clubs are used for different distances. A golfer chooses the right club based on its loft—the angle of the club head. All club heads (except those on putters) are angled. A club with a low loft will hit the ball long and low. A club with a higher loft will send the ball traveling higher, but not as far.

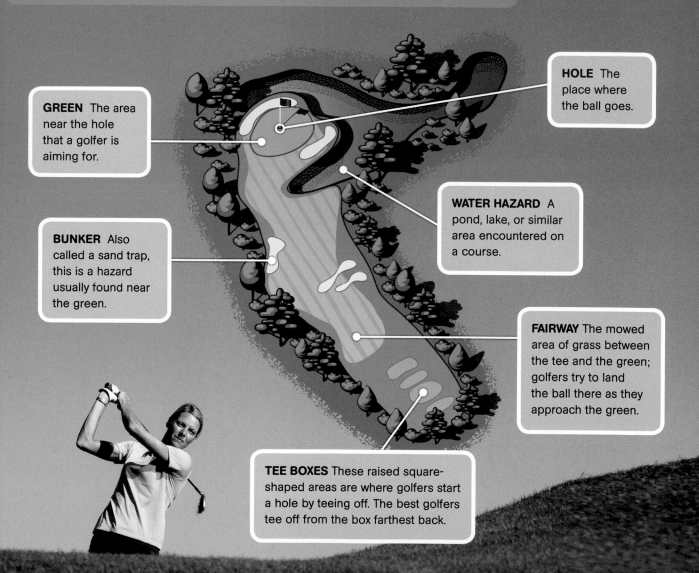

HOLE The place where the ball goes.

GREEN The area near the hole that a golfer is aiming for.

WATER HAZARD A pond, lake, or similar area encountered on a course.

BUNKER Also called a sand trap, this is a hazard usually found near the green.

FAIRWAY The mowed area of grass between the tee and the green; golfers try to land the ball there as they approach the green.

TEE BOXES These raised square-shaped areas are where golfers start a hole by teeing off. The best golfers tee off from the box farthest back.

1 Woods are so named because they were originally made from wood. Persimmon was the preferred type of wood used to make the clubs. Today's "woods" are metal. They are the largest and longest clubs in the set and are used to hit the ball long distances. Golfers use them for the drive—the first shot on a hole. Woods have large, hollow heads.

3 Numbered from one to nine, irons have flat heads that contain grooves. The higher the number on the iron, the steeper the loft. The general rule is to use a lower-numbered iron when far from the hole and a higher-numbered iron as the distance decreases.

2 The biggest wood is the driver. It has a very large club head and a nearly flat face. Players use it for their first shot on the longest holes.

4 When close to the green, a golfer wants the ball to travel high, but not roll far after it lands. That's where wedges come in: a golfer uses one to "chip" the ball toward the green. A special sand wedge is used to blast the ball out of a bunker or sand trap.

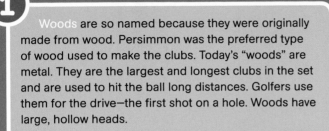

5 Once a golfer is on the green, out comes the putter. This flat-bladed club is made in hundreds of shapes and sizes. Using a soft, easy stroke, the player knocks the flat side of the putter into the ball, aiming to hit the ball directly into the cup, which can be the hardest part of the game.

HOW do ice-skaters spin so fast?

When figure skaters glide onto the ice, they perform beautiful jumps, twists, and turns. One of the most exciting parts of a skating program is the spins. A skater starts her spins slowly and ends up looking like a blur. The faster the skater spins, the more she wows the audience—and the judges. There are all kinds of spins. In one kind, the skater spins in a sitting position. In another, the skater stays upright and may bend her back. In a spin called the camel, the skater spins on one leg while the other leg sticks straight out in a horizontal position.

Some skaters spin faster than others. They look like they're digging holes in the ice! Swiss skating great Lucinda Ruh set a world record in 2003 by spinning 155 times on one foot—without stopping! Polish-Canadian skater Olivia Oliver set a world record in 2015 by spinning at a speed of 342 spins per minute.

1 When a skater starts spinning, she holds her arms and legs away from her body. Like the Earth, she rotates on an axis. The skater's axis is the vertical line that goes from the top of her head to the blade of her skate.

2 The skater begins to move her arms and legs toward her body. That's because the closer her arms and legs are to the axis, the faster she spins.

3 She spins fastest when her arms and legs are tight against her body. A figure skater can control the exact speed of a spin by carefully controlling the movements of her arms and legs.

Did You Know?

The largest outdoor ice rink in the world is located in Japan. The Fujikyu Highland Promenade Rink has an ice area of 165,750 square feet—equal to 3.8 acres.

4 The skater slows and eventually stops the spin by letting her arms and legs move back out. The farther they are from the axis, the slower she spins.

OTHER WAYS TO SPIN

The International Skating Union recognizes eight types of spins—some of which are done from a standing position. In a camel spin, the skater spins on one foot and keeps the body horizontal. A sit spin is also done on one foot, while the skater sits with the other leg stuck out in front. Another standing spin is the layback, in which the skater arches backward.

Camel spin

Beillmann spin

Sit spin

THE DIZZY FACTOR Spin around in place really fast and you get dizzy. You can hardly stand up. So how do figure skaters not get dizzy and not fall down when they spin 30 or 40 times in a few seconds? Well, most skaters do get dizzy. In professional ice skating, there is a small light at both ends of the rink. This helps dizzy skaters figure out where they are at the end of a spin. Some skaters say they just get used to the dizziness. After a while, it doesn't bother them. Some say that if everything around them is a blur, they are less aware of the spin and don't get dizzy. Others just enjoy spinning—they think it's relaxing!

Triple axel jump

HOW does sports equipment keep you safe?

In sports in which bodies collide, athletes wear pads and other specially made protective gear to keep them from getting injured. Football is one of the hardest-hitting sports, with collisions happening all over the field on nearly every play. Modern football gear is designed to keep players safer than ever.

A concussion is a serious brain injury caused by blows, or even a single blow, to the head. Because football is a heavy-contact sport, there is concern that too many players are getting concussions while playing. While helmets have never been better at protecting the head, it's unlikely that any helmet design will be able to eliminate concussions from football completely.

UPPER BODY Most hits in football involve the shoulders. Every player wears a set of shoulder pads that includes pads for the chest and back as well. The layers of the shoulder pads—made of foam covered in hard plastic—absorb the energy of knocks and tackles.

ON THE SIDE Hip pads cover the area where the hard hip bone can be felt under the skin.

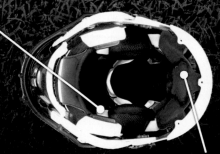

HEADS UP

The outer shell is made of hard plastic. Small holes let hot air escape and help keep the player cool.

A chinstrap holds the helmet securely to the head. A player is required to "strap up" before each play.

The face mask is made of metal covered in rubber or plastic. It is screwed to the helmet and keeps hits (and fingers and the ball) from smacking into a player's face.

Jaw pads are located inside the helmet. They protect the ear, jaw, and side of a player's face.

Inside the helmet is a series of pads that are filled with air after a player puts the helmet on. The inflated pads make the helmet fit snugly. The pads absorb much of the energy produced by blows to the head.

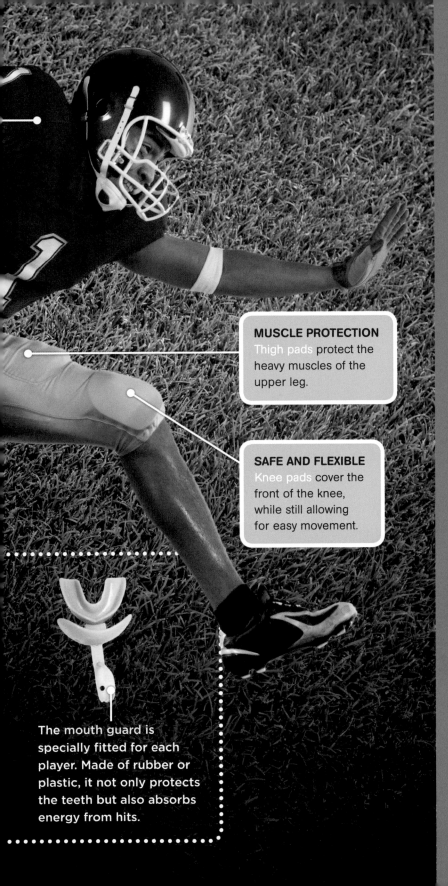

MUSCLE PROTECTION
Thigh pads protect the heavy muscles of the upper leg.

SAFE AND FLEXIBLE
Knee pads cover the front of the knee, while still allowing for easy movement.

The mouth guard is specially fitted for each player. Made of rubber or plastic, it not only protects the teeth but also absorbs energy from hits.

HOW DO OTHER ATHLETES PLAY IT SAFE?

Ice hockey
Players wear pads from head to toe. Helmets are a must. Most players wear plastic face shields. Goalies wear face masks that often look like wire cages.

Motocross
Riders wear full-face helmets, heavy shin guards, padded gloves, and chest protectors.

Baseball A batter wears a hard plastic helmet of carbon fiber shell. A catcher wears a metal mask, a cup, a chest protector, and shin and knee guards. Even umpires get help—a plate ump wears a mask, a chest protector, and steel-toed shoes.

HOW do skiers train?

It takes more than great snow to make great skiers! Skiers train year-round to keep in shape for races. Plus, they practice skills that help them zip down courses. In a sport in which milliseconds matter, they look for every edge, on and off the snow.

Did You Know?

Inline skating uses a lot of the same muscles and movements as skiing. It can help skiers stay strong in the summer.

ACTION Watch great skiers maneuver the slopes and see how stable they keep their upper bodies. From the waist down, however, it's all action. The upper legs twist and turn, pointing the skis in the right direction.

CONTROL Snow may look smooth, but it's not. A skier's knees act like shock absorbers, bending a little over the bumps. The legs control turning.

POSITION It's important for skiers to angle their skis correctly when making fast turns. Drills help them train their ankles to fine-tune that movement.

TRAINING TIPS

Skiers do drills to hone their skills. Gold medalist Mikaela Shiffrin, shown racing at left, reportedly spends more than half her practice time training. Check out these ways skiers train.

Skiers do exercises off the slopes to improve their balance. Holding a one-leg stand is harder than it looks. This pose and other yoga poses improve balance.

Skiing is an aerobic sport—it requires the body to use lots of energy—so skiers spend time training their hearts and lungs. They run, ride exercise bicycles, and use treadmills.

Skiers stretch regularly to keep their muscles limber, because flexibility is vital to the sport. Some skiers do Pilates, a form of exercise that combines strength and flexibility training.

Skiing requires strong legs. Weight training is a big part of off-season workouts. Skiers also do "explosive" movements to build muscle and mimic what their legs do on the slopes. Lunges, box jumps, or step-ups help keep the legs in top form.

HOW do bicycle gears make you go faster?

A bicycle is a great way to get around. It doesn't pollute, it's easy to ride, it's good exercise, and it's fun. One of the best things about a bike is that you can make the ride smoother with the press of a lever. What allows you to get in gear is, well, the gears.

A gear is a wheel with teeth that stick out. A bicycle has two sets of gears. One set is connected to the pedals, the other is attached to the rear wheel. A three-speed bike has three gears. A mountain bike might have 24 gears. These gears let you change the distance the bike travels forward each time you turn the pedals. The higher the gear you put the bike in, the more distance you can travel with each turn of the pedals—and the faster you can go.

FIXIES Some brave cyclists pedal bikes with just one gear and no brakes. Known as fixies (for "fixed-gear bicycles"), these bikes don't change gears. The riders must always keep pedaling (no coasting!). To brake, they stop pedaling or pedal backwards. Enthusiasts choose these bikes for several reasons: the bikes are trendy, low-maintenance, easy to maneuver in city traffic, and just plain awesome to ride. They do, however, require a highly skilled rider.

The front derailleur (derailer) changes the front gears by moving the chain from one gear to another.

The chain turns the rear gears. As the gears turn, so does the back wheel.

The rear derailleur (derailer) changes the back gears by moving the chain from gear to gear.

The chain connects the front and rear gears.

The gears are wheels with cogs, or teeth, that fit into the chain. As the gears spin, so does the chain.

The crank turns the front gears.

The pedals turn the crank.

GEARING UP The higher the gear, the farther the bike goes each time it's pedaled. If the front gear on a bike is twice as big as the rear gear, the rear wheel will turn two times each time you pedal once. If the front gear is three times bigger than the back gear, the back wheel will turn three times for each turn of the pedals. Bicyclists have to pedal harder in high gears, but they can go faster. Riders use high gears to go down hills or speed up on straightaways. In lower gears, riders don't need to pedal as hard, but they can't go as fast as in high gear. Riders use low gears to go up hills.

Rear gears

Front gears

HOW does an arena change an ice rink into a basketball court?

Ice hockey and basketball are very different sports. Hockey players bang into each other as they skate on ice. Basketball players run and jump on a wooden floor.

Even though the games and playing surfaces are very different, the sports are often played in the same arena— and on the same day! How do workers make the changeover? Here's how they do it in STAPLES Center in Los Angeles, California.

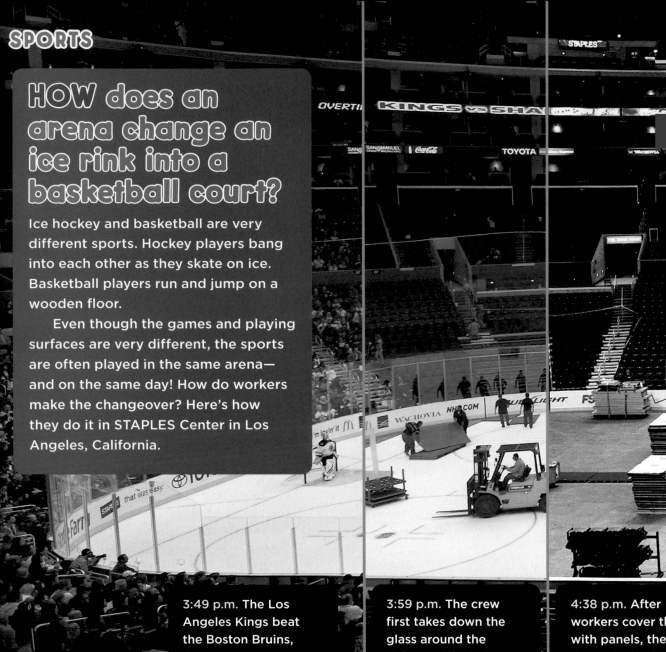

3:49 p.m. The Los Angeles Kings beat the Boston Bruins, 4–3. The game went into overtime, so the STAPLES Center workers have less time than usual to get ready for the Los Angeles Clippers NBA game, which is set to start in less than four hours.

3:59 p.m. The crew first takes down the glass around the rink. Forklifts help remove the glass and the pieces that hold the glass in place. Then workers begin to cover the ice with more than 600 panels, which protect the ice surface and help keep it frozen.

4:38 p.m. After workers cover the ice with panels, they put down the basketball floor. They start at center court and build outward. The basketball court is made of 217 pieces. The pieces are numbered and come out stacked on top of one another.

Did You Know?

In 2014, the Cleveland Cavaliers hoisted one of the largest arena scoreboards in the world to the top of Quicken Loans Arena. The two screens facing the sidelines are each more than 55 feet wide and more than 30 feet high. The entire massive structure includes more than 5,000 square feet of video screens.

4:57 p.m. The crew cleans dust off the floor with a special solution. At the same time, the netting around the rink is lifted to the ceiling. The crew also removes the penalty boxes and team benches that were used in the hockey game. For basketball, workers add another 80 seats.

5:23 p.m. TV crews and photographers begin to set up their cameras when the floor is three-quarters complete. The overhead scoreboard, called a jumbotron, is switched from hockey to basketball graphics.

7:44 p.m. The game between the Los Angeles Clippers and the Cleveland Cavaliers starts in front of a full house. The STAPLES Center crew makes this changeover about 200 times a year. That's why these veterans need such a short time to turn an icy rink into a hardwood court.

FINE FORESTS

Nearly every NBA floor is made from maple wood grown in Michigan and Wisconsin. Teams are required to change their floors every 10 years, and just three companies provide most of the wood. Only the Boston Celtics play on a different type of wood—red oak.

49

HOW TO
play pickup basketball

All you need for a pickup game of basketball is a group of kids and a place to play ball. Of course, you can play pickup games of other sports, too. Organize a soccer match on a field or even play at the beach. Or, if there's room, mark out a diamond and have a game of kickball or baseball. The key is for everyone to work as one team . . . until the game starts. Then, may the best team win.

What you need:

- Players
- Basketball
- A basketball hoop
- Water to stay hydrated

What to do:

1 Get together with other players. You can gather your own friends to play, or find a pickup game at a local school or rec center.

2 Find a place to play regularly. Your school may offer after-school court time outdoors or in the gym. Or, if you are lucky enough to have a friend who has a hoop, make plans to meet at his or her house.

3 Pick teams. There are many ways to pick teams. Two captains can take turns choosing players. Or form teams based on similar characteristics. You can divide up based on the first letter of the players' last names (*A-L* on one team, *M-Z* on another) or split people up based on whether they are wearing a light or dark-colored shirt. If you have an odd number of players, the other players can take turns subbing out, so everyone gets a break during the game.

4 Choose the type of game. With a bigger group, play full-court. If you have eight or fewer players—or only one hoop—try a half-court game. The teams take turns shooting at the same basket. After Team A misses a shot, Team B dribbles or passes the ball back to the half-court line. Then it's their turn to try for a basket. The same thing happens after a team makes a basket—the other team "checks" the ball in at half-court. Full-court play follows the standard rules of basketball.

PRO TIP Call your own fouls. There's no referee for playground games. Instead, players call fouls on themselves when they make them or on an opponent who fouls. Pickup is a game of honesty.

5 Gear up. You don't need expensive basketball shoes for a pickup game; sneakers will do the trick. If you're playing outside, use a rubber basketball; leather balls should only be used indoors. For uniforms, one team can wear dark shirts and the other one light shirts.

6 Play. You can play to any number of points, but 11 or 21 are common. To make the game tougher, use the rule that a team needs to win by two points—that can make for some great late-game action.

CHAPTER 3

BUILDINGS

HOW were the Egyptian pyramids built?

The first pyramid was built in Egypt about 4,000 years ago. Pyramids were tombs for the kings of Egypt, called pharaohs. Hundreds of pyramids were built, and more than 100 still survive. The most famous are in Giza, outside of Cairo, the capital of Egypt.

It took a great deal of skill and tens of thousands of workers to build the pyramids. Experts once thought that slaves had constructed the pyramids, but a recent discovery suggests that paid laborers may have done at least some of the work. A small town was constructed near a pyramid site to house all the workers, the officials in charge, and the people who supplied them with food and materials. Carpenters made tools and built sleds to haul heavy loads. Metalworkers created cutting tools and kept them sharp. Potters formed pots used to prepare food and carry water. Bakers baked bread for the other workers. Together, these different kinds of workers helped build the pyramids—the world's first skyscrapers.

1 Pyramids were built mostly from limestone. The stone was dug out of a quarry—a large open pit. Each block of stone weighed several tons.

2 Before construction began, the base of the pyramid was measured off and sand was removed from the site. A platform, built out of limestone, served as the pyramid's foundation.

3 Groups of men hauled the stone blocks from the quarry to the pyramid site. They used ropes and levers made of wood to lift the blocks onto heavy sleds. If the quarry was far from the pyramid, workers or oxen would pull the sleds to the Nile River, a distance of up to five miles. From there, barges would carry the blocks to the building site.

Humans are builders. Over thousands of years, people have created incredible structures. From tombs to canals, engineering wonders continue to amaze us.

6 Workers placed a capstone, a small pyramid-shaped stone, at the top of the pyramid. Some capstones were covered with gold or other shiny metals to reflect the rays of the sun.

MAKING A POINT Other ancient civilizations built pyramids, too. Here are a few examples.

The Pyramid of the Sun is located not far from Mexico City. The vast structure was built by an ancient people of Mexico called the Teotihuacanos (tay-oh-tee-*wha*-cahn-oz) nearly 2,000 years ago. At 246 feet tall and 733 feet wide on each side, it is the third-largest pyramid in the world.

5 Stones that formed steps made up the central core of the pyramid. Small, soft stones filled in the spaces between the steps. A layer of fine limestone was placed against the small stones to make the outside of the pyramid smooth. This outer layer was removed centuries ago, and the stone was used to build Cairo.

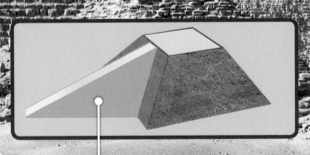

There are many Hindu temples shaped like pyramids in India. One, the Brihadisvara Temple in Thanjavur, was built in the 11th century. Made of granite, the temple tower is 216 feet high.

4 The workers hauled blocks up a ramp onto the pyramid. There may have been a single long ramp or several smaller ones. Experts are still learning about this part of the construction process.

HOW does a suspension bridge stay up?

Suspension bridges span long distances, such as rivers and canyons. They are called suspension bridges because their bridge decks (the roadway where cars and people cross) hang from cables. The word *suspend* means "to hang something." The cables hang from other cables strung between two towers, which keep the bridge stable and upright. The series of hanging cables supports the massive weight of the bridge. Engineers calculate that weight to make sure the bridge is strong enough. They also design the bridge so it can sway in the wind without collapsing.

Constructing a suspension bridge is complicated. Here's how it's done.

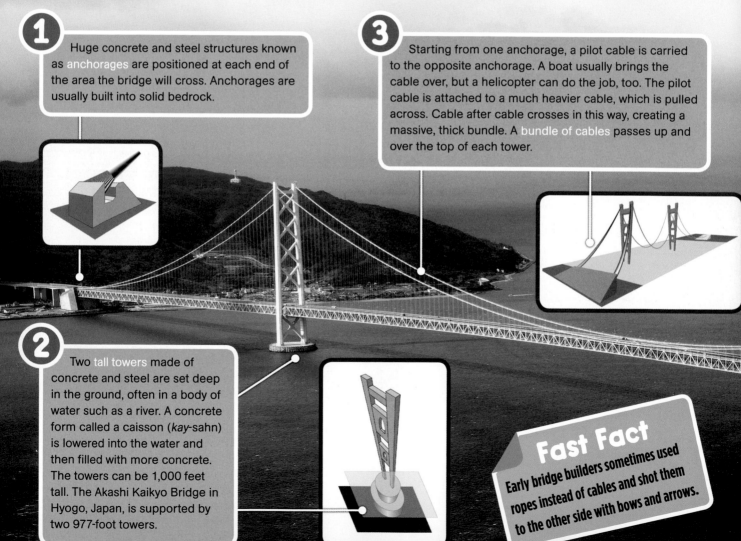

1 Huge concrete and steel structures known as anchorages are positioned at each end of the area the bridge will cross. Anchorages are usually built into solid bedrock.

2 Two tall towers made of concrete and steel are set deep in the ground, often in a body of water such as a river. A concrete form called a caisson (*kay*-sahn) is lowered into the water and then filled with more concrete. The towers can be 1,000 feet tall. The Akashi Kaikyo Bridge in Hyogo, Japan, is supported by two 977-foot towers.

3 Starting from one anchorage, a pilot cable is carried to the opposite anchorage. A boat usually brings the cable over, but a helicopter can do the job, too. The pilot cable is attached to a much heavier cable, which is pulled across. Cable after cable crosses in this way, creating a massive, thick bundle. A bundle of cables passes up and over the top of each tower.

Fast Fact
Early bridge builders sometimes used ropes instead of cables and shot them to the other side with bows and arrows.

TOP 5 WORLD'S LONGEST SUSPENSION BRIDGES

BRIDGE	LOCATION	LENGTH (FEET)	OPENED
1. Akashi Kaikyo	Japan	6,532	1998
2. Xihoumen Waterway	China	5,413	2009
3. Great East Belt	Denmark	5,328	1998
4. Osman Gazi	Turkey	5,085	2017
5. Yu-Sun Sin	South Korea	5,069	2013

5 Working from both ends at once, the builders hang a grid of metal (the bridge deck) from the wires. It's a tricky task: Two sets of builders have to work at the same pace so the two sides of the deck stay the same weight. Eventually, the workers meet in the middle.

6 Once the deck is in place, the construction workers lay down roadway and install electric wires for lights and signals.

Akashi Kaikyo Bridge

4 Bridge builders hang wires from the two main bridge cables.

7 The bridge is complete. Welcome, cars and pedestrians!

BUILDINGS

HOW does the Panama Canal work?

The Panama Canal is one big ditch. This 300-foot-wide, 48-mile-long channel cuts through the nation of Panama, in Central America, and connects the Atlantic and Pacific Oceans. Before the canal was completed in 1914, ships had to travel around the tip of South America to go from New York to California. The Panama Canal shortens that trip by 8,000 miles.

Most of the Panama Canal is above sea level, so ships that pass through it must be raised and lowered by a series of devices called locks. Today, about 14,000 ships sail through the Panama Canal each year. In 2016, the canal reopened after a major upgrade. Locks and channels were widened to let enormous cargo ships sail through. The trip through the canal takes about eight to 10 hours.

Atlantic Ocean

Panama

Pacific Ocean

Gatun Lake

Atlantic Ocean

1 A ship that enters the Panama Canal from the Atlantic Ocean begins its journey at Limon Bay.

2 The ship sails at sea level for 6.5 miles to the Gatun Locks. There, three separate chambers raise the ship about 85 feet. Now the ship is at the level of Gatun Lake.

3 The water that pours into the Panama Canal's locks flows from Gatun Lake through special pipes. The ship is at its highest point as it sails about 23 miles across the lake.

4 From Gatun Lake, the ship enters the Gaillard Cut, an eight-mile-long channel.

HOW A LOCK WORKS When a ship in a canal needs to be raised, it enters a lock. Locks are giant compartments made of thick concrete walls, with huge metal doors at each end. One door opens for the ship to enter, then closes behind it. Water flows into the compartment, and the ship rises with it. The lock continues to flood until its water level is the same as that of the higher lock ahead of it. Then the front door opens and the ship sails through it into the next lock. Each lock lifts the ship higher and higher. Locks can lower ships, too. When a ship enters a lock, the water is pumped out until the ship is at a lower level. Other locks lower the ship more and more.

Miraflores Lake

Pacific Ocean

5 At the end of the Gaillard Cut, the ship enters the Pedro Miguel Locks. The lock lowers the ship about 30 feet into Miraflores Lake.

6 A two-mile-long channel leads the ship to the two Miraflores Locks. They lower the ship to sea level. It takes about seven minutes for water to enter or drain from the locks. The ship sails seven miles until it reaches the Pacific Ocean.

Fast Fact

Several people have passed through the Panama Canal without a boat . . . by swimming! The most famous canal swimmer was Richard Halliburton, who accomplished this feat in 1928. Because the canal charges by weight, Halliburton paid only 36 cents to have the locks opened and closed for him. He swam a total of 50 hours over 10 days.

57

HOW was Mount Rushmore built?

The four heads carved on Mount Rushmore, located in the Black Hills of South Dakota, are big shots in every way. The heads of presidents George Washington, Thomas Jefferson, Theodore Roosevelt, and Abraham Lincoln are each 60 feet tall.

Sculptor Gutzon Borglum began the project in 1927, and it was completed in 1941. During that time, workers removed 450,000 tons of granite (a type of stone) from Mount Rushmore, mostly by dynamite. Workers used dynamite and other tools to help create one of the largest works of art in the world.

Fast Fact

The original plan was to show each president down to the waist (as seen in the model below). But it took so long and cost so much that construction stopped after the heads were finished.

1 Mount Rushmore was picked because granite is easy to carve. Also, the mountainside receives a lot of sunlight, so visitors would be able to view it for most of the day.

2 Borglum made a small model of the four presidents. Each inch on the model represented one foot on the mountain. Workers used the model to create the sculpture on the mountain.

3 Workers prepared dynamite charges. The dynamite removed rock to within three or four inches of the finished faces, creating the shapes of lips, cheeks, noses, necks, and brows.

Did You Know?

Each nose is 20 feet long, each mouth is 18 feet wide, and each eye is 11 feet across. If the presidents' bodies were built to scale, they would be 46 stories high.

6 As Mount Rushmore neared completion in 1941, workers used hammers and chisels to smooth the rock faces.

4 Men worked on the side of the mountain while sitting in leather seats attached to steel cables. Hand-cranked winches raised and lowered the workers.

5 Before the final stages, drillers made many small holes in the granite. They then wedged off the granite between the holes, exposing the final layer of rock.

59

HOW is a skyscraper built?

A skyscraper stays upright the same way you do: with the help of a skeleton. Instead of being made of bone, a skyscraper's skeleton is made of steel. Engineers build the steel skeleton. They create different patterns of steel frames and bars—sometimes covered and reinforced with concrete. Once the skeleton is in place, walls and floors are added around it, completing the massive building.

1 Every skyscraper fits a specific footprint (the area where a building stands). After the building's owner chooses how tall the building will be, an architect creates a plan to make a building of that height that fits the specified footprint.

2 Working with computer programs and testing models in wind tunnels, the architect and engineers make sure the building won't fall down. They test the design to ensure that the real building can withstand high winds, earthquakes, and other stresses.

3 Construction work on a skyscraper starts at the bottom, where workers dig a huge pit that will become the building's foundation. A frame inside the pit holds back the soil. Huge columns are blasted into the bedrock to support the weight of the whole building.

4 Starting at the foundation, workers form the skeleton, using long steel beams. They follow the architect's plan carefully, connecting the beams by welding them together. Some very tall skyscrapers also have central steel and concrete cores to which their outer skeletons are attached.

5 How do those beams get where they need to be? A crane that rises higher and higher as the building goes up helps put the beams in place. Workers attach a cable to a beam on the ground, and the crane operator carefully lifts the beam to the correct floor.

TOP 5 TALLEST SKYSCRAPERS

SKYSCRAPER	LOCATION	HEIGHT (FEET)	COMPLETED
1. Burj Khalifa	Dubai, United Arab Emirates	2,717	2010
2. Shanghai Tower	Shanghai, China	2,073	2015
3. Makkah Royal Clock Tower Hotel	Mecca, Saudi Arabia	1,972	2012
4. Ping An Finance Center	Shenzhen, China	1,965	2017
5. Lotte World Tower	Seoul, South Korea	1,819	2017

6 As the skeleton takes shape, work begins on the floors.

7 As the floors are finished, the outside is added. The buildings are designed not only to look beautiful, but also to help with energy efficiency and wind safety and to meet local building rules. Most skyscraper designs use lots of glass, but they can also include metal panels, concrete structures, or sections of stone.

8 Inside, workers scurry to install water lines, electrical cables, Internet and computer connections, heating and air conditioning, and of course, elevators—because no one wants to walk up 100 floors every morning!

HOW TO
pitch a tent

The days of leaky canvas tents and knot tying are long gone! Today's tents are made of sturdy, lightweight nylon and are fairly simple to set up. You do, however, have to pitch a tent correctly if you want to have a safe, dry place to sleep while on a campout.

There are different tent structures. It's important to read the manufacturer's instructions that come with your tent—before you go camping. Practice pitching your tent in your yard in advance of your outing. Here's a step-by-step guide to setting up a common tent type.

What you need:

- A tent (including poles and stakes)
- A tarp (a large sheet of strong, waterpoof plastic)
- A stake mallet (or rock)

Tent Tips

☀ Zip your tent when you leave it—this habit keeps bugs out and warm air in.

☀ Have a flashlight handy in case you need to pitch the tent at night.

☀ Put all poles and stakes in one bag so they don't get lost.

☀ Leave a "front porch" area where you can keep shoes. This way, you don't track dirt into your temporary home.

☀ Choose a camping spot at the top of a hill; sites downhill can get soaked when it rains.

What to do:

1 Find a flat, dry spot. Clear away branches, pinecones, rocks, and anything else you don't want to sleep on. Use a tarp—slightly bigger than the tent floor—to cover the ground. Spread the tarp flat.

2 Unroll and lay out the tent, bottom side down, on the tarp.

3 Open out the flexible poles and slide one through the loops on top of the tent, moving from one corner to the opposite one. Repeat this process with the other pole so that it crosses the first one.

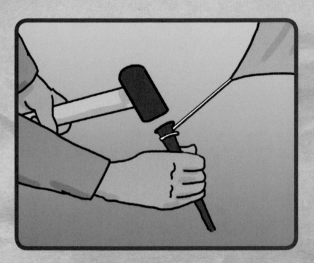

5 Center the tent on the tarp. Pound the tent stakes into the ground, connecting them to the ties at each corner. Check that the stakes are firmly in place so the tent is secure.

4 With a partner, put the ends of the poles into the metal grommets or pockets of webbing at each corner of the tent. The last corner will be the hardest. The poles are flexible, but you'll still need a little muscle to get them in place.

6 The rain fly—or roof—goes above or around the tent. Your tent should have loops or ties that connect it to the rain fly, which should sit a few inches above the top of the tent. Always secure the rain fly.

CHAPTER 4

SCIENCE

HOW do robots know what to do?

How do robots know how to build a car, stock a warehouse shelf, or vacuum your bedroom floor? The answer lies in the similarities between robotic design and the human body. Like a human, a robot needs a "brain"—in this case, a computer—that can be programmed to perform different functions. Computer programmers break each specific task into several steps. The computer then directs small motors called actuators, which are located at different parts of the robot's body. While muscles move human limbs, actuators move wheels, pistons, and gears. Many robots are equipped with sensors that allow them to track the distances their joints have moved, their locations in environments, and even the pressure they are putting on objects.

Different types of actuators can be used to move the parts of a robot. One type of electric motor is called a stepper motor, named for the way it rotates in small increments, or steps.

The handlike claw, or gripper, is programmed to do a particular task. It may tighten screws, hold a paint sprayer, or move things from place to place.

Did You Know?

The International Space Station (ISS) has a robotic arm that is 57.7 feet long. It moves equipment into place, captures unpiloted spacecraft carrying supplies, and has assisted astronauts during spacewalks. The arm can be controlled by the crew on board the space station or from ISS mission control at Johnson Space Center in Houston, Texas.

Like human arms, robotic arms have joints. Each joint has a motor.

To understand what powers our homes, how icebergs form, and how gravity works, you need science. Every day, scientists learn more about how our world works.

MECHATRONICS

Mecha comes from "mechanical" and *tronics* from "electronics." Combined with computer science, mechatronic technology is increasingly used in product development and manufacturing.

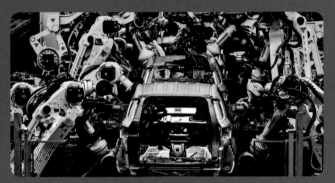

CAR PARTS Industrial robots assemble, package, and label products—even items as large as cars. As of 2015, the Ford Motor Company was using 20,000 robots in factories around the world. Some are equipped with lasers that act as "eyes," scanning vehicles to make sure doors, windshields, and fenders are installed correctly.

LEARNED BEHAVIOR Scientists can now create robots that respond to their environments. A feature called reactive control allows a robot to respond to external signals and change its behavior accordingly—for instance, altering course if it recognizes an object in its path. Some can change behaviors based on experiences.

HELPING HANDS Robots can be programmed to assist in many ways. Rory A. Cooper designed the Personal Mobility and Manipulation Appliance (PerMMA) to help people with disabilities perform everyday tasks. Its two robotic arms can be controlled using a touchpad, microphone, or joystick. It can also be controlled remotely by an assistant.

GETTING AROUND Robots move on wheels, treads, or even legs. Because search-and-rescue robots with two legs are often unstable, designers usually equip them with at least four. In 2017, however, a robotics team from the University of Oregon unveiled an agile two-legged robot named Cassie that can stand, handle difficult terrain and changes in elevation, and resist water damage. Cassie could be used for search-and-rescue operations in the future.

HOW does an iceberg form?

Glaciers are huge masses of ice that move very slowly over land. A chunk of ice that breaks off a glacier and floats across the sea is called an iceberg. Many icebergs originate in the North Atlantic Ocean. Every year, between 15,000 and 30,000 icebergs calve, or break off, from glaciers in Greenland, in the North Atlantic. The *Titanic* was a British ship that sank when it collided with an iceberg in the North Atlantic in 1912. A smaller number of icebergs form in Alaska, while some of the biggest break off from Antarctic ice shelves. One Antarctic iceberg was the size of Connecticut!

1 An iceberg starts out as snow falling on land. As more snow falls over thousands of years, the snow at the top packs down the flakes at the bottom.

2 Over the centuries, the packed-down snow becomes ice, which can grow to be hundreds of miles long and thousands of feet thick. This sheet of ice, known as a glacier, slowly moves forward under the force of its own weight.

COOL CUSTOMERS Just-born bergs begin large—if floating ice isn't at least 98 feet thick, it isn't considered an iceberg. But most melt away in a few months. Some melt down into growlers, which are icebergs that are about as big as pianos. Slightly larger ones, called bergy bits, are about the size of small houses. Icebergs come in all kinds of shapes and colors. Tabular icebergs are shaped like tables, with flat tops and steep sides. Tabular icebergs are very large. Non-tabular icebergs can have rounded tops (dome iceberg), pointy parts (pinnacle berg), slots cut through by water (dry-dock berg), or just about any other odd shape formed by melting ice.

Growler

Bergy bit

TRUE BLUE? Most icebergs are transparent. But they look white because air bubbles in the ice reflect visible light wavelengths equally. An iceberg can look blue, too, because it is made of thick ice. When glacial ice is compressed, air bubbles are squeezed out. The dense ice absorbs and reflects light differently, giving the iceberg a blue color. Algae, bits of rock, and sea life in the ice can cause green or yellow bergs.

3 The glacier, moving forward at a rate of up to six feet a day, eventually reaches the sea.

Tabular iceberg

Dome iceberg

Pinnacle berg

Dry-dock berg

4 As the end of the glacier moves out past the land, the ice calves into the sea. The chunks that fall into the water are icebergs.

HOW do scientists uncover and remove fossils from a dig?

Scientists who study the life of the past are called paleontologists (pay-lee-ahn-*tah*-lo-jists). They learn about prehistoric times by digging up and studying fossils, which are the remains of ancient plants and animals. Most fossils are bones and teeth—the hardest parts of an animal.

Finding fossils isn't easy. Scientists might walk slowly for days across deserts, through canyons, over hills, or along riverbanks, looking at rocks. They keep their eyes peeled for a slightly different color that stands out from its surroundings—this might be a prehistoric bone. Once scientists discover a bone, they try to figure out what kind of animal it belonged to. That's not always simple, because the fossils might be very tiny or broken. When scientists do find a fossil that interests them, the real work begins: removing it from the rock.

Paleontologists dig out dinosaur fossils from a vertical wall at Dinosaur National Monument, located in Utah and Colorado.

It's important that paleontologists make accurate notes on the dimensions, locations, and other details of the bones they find. When they get back to the lab, this information helps them determine where and when the creature might have lived.

1 After a fossil is discovered, scientists use picks to gently dig away a block of rock around it. They clear away the rock fragments with a brush. If the bone is easily breakable, it is covered in liquid glue to harden it.

2 As scientists cut around the fossil, they wrap both the delicate bone and the surrounding rock in a protective jacket. A jacket is made of strips of burlap drenched in plaster. The strips are layered over the fossil, then coated with more plaster.

3 After the plaster cast dries, workers lift it from the ground and carry it to a vehicle. Some casts are so heavy, trucks or even helicopters are needed to take them from the site.

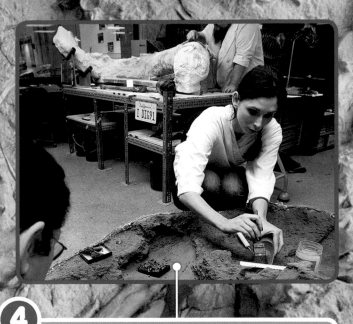

4 The cast is sent to a lab at a museum or university. There, researchers cut off the plaster and remove rock from the bones with tools such as brushes and grinders. They clean the bone and glue it back together if it is broken.

HOW does a combine harvester make wheat and straw?

Have you ever wondered how a field of grain—like wheat, barley, or rye—is turned into food for people? We eat only the edible seeds of grain crops—sometimes whole, like oats, and sometimes after they've been milled into flour and baked into bread. Separating edible seeds from their inedible outer casings (chaff) and lower stems (straw) is the key to turning grains into food. It is a difficult and time-consuming task. But a combine harvester can do it all. It is so named because it combines the three steps of harvesting grain: cutting, threshing, and winnowing.

3 Screws and conveyors move the cut crops farther into the combine and deposit them into a threshing drum, where grains and stalks are separated.

2 A wheel pushes the crops against a cutter bar.

1 The combine drives over crops, and the header gathers them.

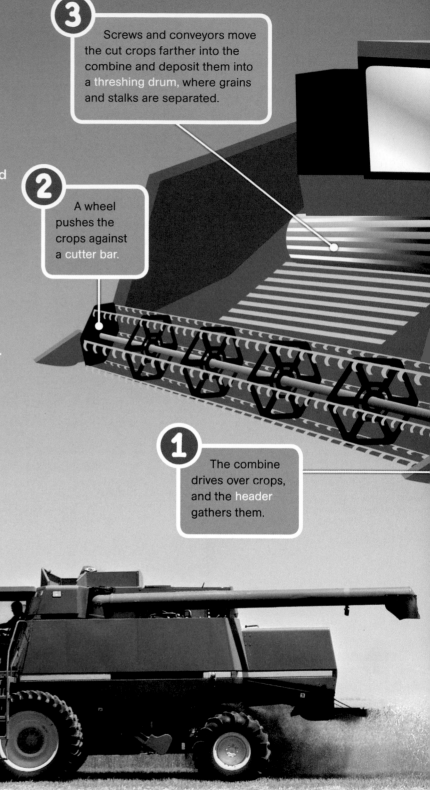

Fast Fact

American Hiram Moore invented the combine in the 1830s. It took more than a dozen horses to operate. Later models used steam power. The Holt Company of California outfitted a combine with a gas-powered engine in 1911.

4 A winnowing fan helps separate grains from straw. Grains and plant material are filtered through sieves.

5 Unwanted straw is sent out the back of the combine and clean grains are saved in tanks.

Handy work
Before the invention of threshing machines, people cut grain with handheld blades called scythes. Plants were pounded to separate seeds and stalks in a process known as threshing. Winnowing is the task of removing the husks around the seeds by shaking the grains into the air so that the chaff blows away. A combine is an expensive farm machine, and some farmers still do the work by hand today.

Threshing grain by hand

THEY DO IT ALL
Combines are multi-functional machines. They harvest corn with attachments called corn heads. Inside the combine, fast-spinning rotors separate the kernels and send them to a storage tank. Cobs and husks are dropped back onto the field. With different attachments, combines harvest sugar beets and deposit them in large mounds in the field, where they are gathered by the truckload. Some models are designed to harvest grapes. And others do the backbreaking work of picking cotton.

Corn

Beets

Grapes

Cotton

HOW do light bulbs work?

Every evening, the sun sets, and without sources of light it is difficult to cook, be social, do homework, or do other tasks around the home. For thousands of years, humans used fire to illuminate their environments. Many ancient civilizations—including the Egyptians, the Romans, and the Chinese during the Qin Dynasty—used wax or tallow candles with wicks. Humans had to make do with candlelight until British inventors showed in 1835 that electric light was possible using an arc lamp. That paved the way for the invention of the electric light bulb.

1 American inventor Thomas Edison patented the first electric bulb in 1879. It was known as an incandescent bulb. An incandescent bulb contains a wire called a filament. When electricity heats the filament to a very high temperature, it produces light. Edison's first bulb used a carbon filament and burned for a little over 13 hours. Other inventors experimented with different filament materials, including tungsten, that last for longer periods of time. Incandescent bulbs are cheap to make and come in many sizes. On the downside, they use lots of energy, burn out quickly compared to other bulbs, and have a negative impact on the environment.

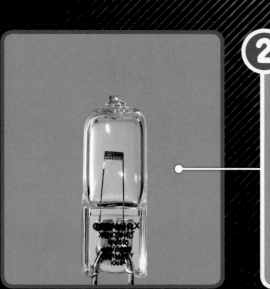

2 In 1955, two inventors from General Electric in Ohio developed a stronger, longer-lasting version of the incandescent bulb called a halogen bulb. A halogen bulb is filled with halogen gas. Due to a chemical reaction between the halogen and the metal filament inside, the bulb burns longer, brighter, and more efficiently than an incandescent light bulb. Because of their power, halogen bulbs are often used to light movie sets. The downside of halogen bulbs is their dangerously high temperature, which can cause burns if users touch them. People can transfer their skin oils to the bulbs, which may shatter if the heated oils create too much surface heat.

3
A fluorescent bulb does not have a filament. Instead, it uses gas and a special coating on the inside of the bulb to produce light. The concept behind fluorescent bulbs has been around since the 19th century, but the bulbs did not become available until the 1930s, after many different inventors perfected the technology. Fluorescent bulbs are often used to light large, open spaces, including factories, stores, and tunnels.

4
The compact fluorescent light, or CFL, was invented in the 1970s in response to a widespread energy crisis. CFLs warm up slowly, but they take 70% less energy to run than incandescent bulbs. In a CFL bulb, an electric current runs through a tube filled with argon (a gas) and mercury vapor. When electrons interact with the mercury atoms, ultraviolet light is created. This light is beyond the spectrum of light we normally see. When the ultraviolet light hits a coating on the inside of the tube called a phosphor, it turns visible and begins to glow. Since CFLs don't have filaments, they remain cool and don't burn out as quickly as incandescent bulbs.

5
Light-emitting diodes, or LEDs, are another type of light source. An LED creates light when electrons move in a semiconductor material. Electrons lose energy and that energy is emitted as light. LEDs are expensive, but they burn for a long time—up to 50,000 hours. The first LED of visible light was invented in 1962 by Nick Holonyak, Jr., in Syracuse, New York.

Fast Fact

A patent gives an inventor the sole right to manufacture or sell his or her invention for a period of time. Edison applied for his first patent in 1868, at the age of 21. Over his lifetime, he held 1,093 patents.

HOW are oil spills cleaned up?

In 2010, an explosion on an oil rig in the Gulf of Mexico killed 11 workers and sent oil spewing into the water. Before the leak was plugged, 206 million gallons of oil had flowed into the Gulf, making it the worst oil spill in U.S. history. In an average year, ships and pipelines spill about 1.3 million gallons of oil in U.S. waters.

Oil spills happen for many reasons, from natural disasters such as hurricanes and earthquakes to accidents involving tankers, pipelines, and oil storage tanks. Whatever the cause, oil spills—especially those in the ocean—harm animals and the environment. Because oil spills have become common, more and more ways of cleaning them up have been invented.

BOOMS These long, snakelike tubes float on the water like fences to corral an oil slick and keep it from spreading.

HOW ARE BIRDS CLEANED AFTER AN OIL SPILL?

A veterinarian checks a bird's physical condition and gives the okay for it to be washed. Washing a stressed bird could kill it.

Workers clean the bird's eyes and breathing passages. They wash it in a tub of warm water containing a small amount of dishwashing liquid. The bird then gets a shower of clean water to rinse away soap and oil.

ABSORBERS Spongelike substances called sorbents are dropped into the water to absorb oil. Sorbents can be natural materials like straw or sawdust, or they can be human-made materials. When they have absorbed all they can, the oil-soaked sponges are removed from the water.

BURNING Sometimes an oil slick is set on fire to burn off the oil. But the smoke causes air pollution.

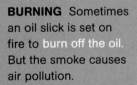

The bird is transferred to a pool of warm water, where it uses its beak to preen, or smooth its feathers. The bird is then put into a pool of cold water to make sure it can float and its feathers are waterproof.

Before releasing the rehabilitated bird, biologists may attach a tag or a radio transmitter to the animal to track its movement and study its behavior.

HOW does gravity work?

No matter where you are on Earth, there's no escaping gravity. Even professional basketball players have to land back on the court after leaping into the air. What goes up must come down.

We know gravity is powerful, but how does it work? All objects that have mass—including you—exert gravitational force. This is the force that pulls objects toward one another, like the basketball player who is pulled toward the ground.

The degree of gravitational force between objects depends on the mass of the objects and how close they are to one another. Small objects with low mass exert weak gravitational force, while larger objects—such as the sun, moon, and planets—have strong gravitational force. When objects are close together, the gravitational pull between them is stronger than when they are far apart.

Isaac Newton was a 17th-century English scientist who figured out how gravity works. The story goes that an apple fell on his head while he was sitting under an apple tree, and he wondered what caused it to drop. He developed the law of universal gravitation, which states that all particles of matter in the universe attract each other in ways that depend on their sizes and distances.

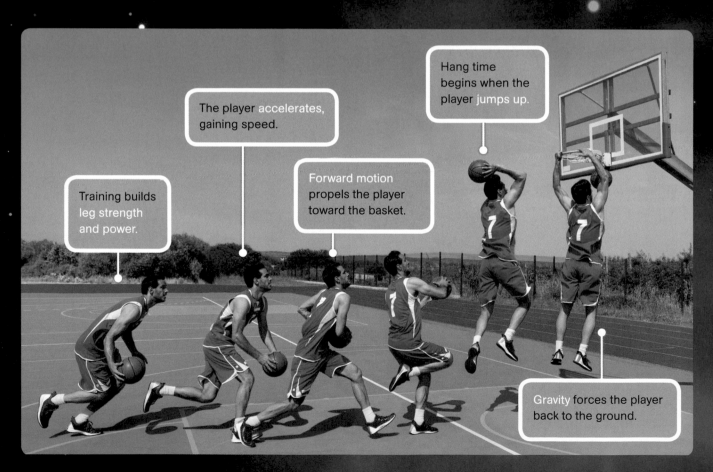

Training builds leg strength and power.

The player accelerates, gaining speed.

Forward motion propels the player toward the basket.

Hang time begins when the player jumps up.

Gravity forces the player back to the ground.

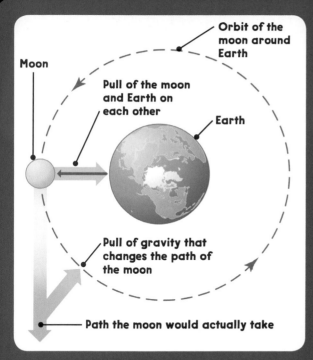

Orbit of the moon around Earth

Moon

Pull of the moon and Earth on each other

Earth

Pull of gravity that changes the path of the moon

Path the moon would actually take

EARTH AND MOON The gravitational pull of the sun keeps Earth orbiting it at just the right distance, giving us the light and heat needed for our survival. The gravitational force of Earth pulls the moon toward Earth's center; this keeps the moon in its orbit and prevents it from moving in a straight line out into space. Even the moon's gravitational pull affects our planet—it influences the oceans, creating the rise and fall of the tides.

Did You Know?

If a bowling ball and a marble were to drop off the top of a building, which would hit the ground first? If you said the bowling ball (because it's heavier), you'd be wrong. Both would land at the same time, assuming there was no air resistance —the speed at which objects fall is the same, no matter their weight.

HEAVY STUFF The terms *mass* and *weight* are sometimes used interchangeably, but they are not the same thing. Weight is the force of gravity acting on an object, while mass is the amount of stuff an object is made of. Your body would have the same mass on the moon as it does on Earth. But because there is less gravitational force on the moon, you would weigh less there. A 100-pound person would weigh just 17 pounds on the moon, and these weights on other planets:

On Mercury: 38 lbs.

On Venus: 91 lbs.

On Earth: 100 lbs.

Sun

On Mars: 38 lbs.

On Jupiter: 253 lbs.

On Saturn: 107 lbs.

On Uranus: 91 lbs.

On Neptune: 114 lbs.

HOW TO use math in everyday life

Math is involved in many parts of your life. If you've ever had to calculate how long it will take you to walk from your house to the bus stop or how many chapters of a book you need to read each night so you can finish a report on time, you've used math in daily life. No matter where you look, numbers and math are everywhere.

What to do:

1 SPORTS
Whether you're trying to hit a home run over the outfield wall, throwing a football 60 yards down the field, or watching the shot clock on the basketball court, numbers count. Here are important numbers on the basketball scoreboard:

* Game score
* Period of play
* Time left in period
* Fouls
* Shot clock (time player has to make a shot)

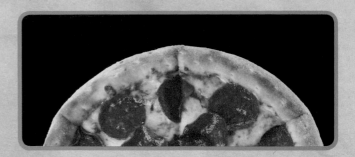

2 FOOD
In restaurants, chefs use math in many ways. They calculate how much food to buy, how much to make, how long it will take to prepare and cook, how many cooks they need, and how much to charge for each dish. Food math matters at home, too. On pizza night, how many pizzas do you need to be sure you have enough slices for everyone? (There may be leftover slices, depending on how many you want.)

Number of people: 8
Number of slices per pizza: 6
People eating two slices: 3
People eating one slice: 4
Number of slices you want: ?

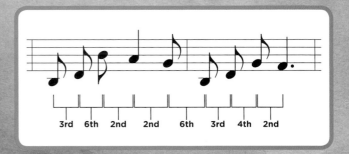

3rd 6th 2nd 2nd 6th 3rd 4th 2nd

3 MUSIC
Musicians use math to interpret scales, chord patterns, rhythm, and timing. A scale spans eight musical notes in ascending or descending order. Notes have different values, such as a whole, a half, and a quarter. Distances between notes (high and low pitches) are described numerically, as shown in the line of music above.

4 **BUILDING** How much wood is needed to build a house? How many nails? How many workers? How long will it take, and how much will it cost? Carpenters and builders use mathematical calculations in their work. If they cut a piece of wood to the wrong length, it's useless, which means wasted time and money. Can you guess what the common builder's expression "measure twice, cut once" means?

5 **GROWING** From backyard gardeners to farmers with acres of crops, growers use math to figure out how many seeds they need, how long it will take for plants to grow, and how many days before harvesting. Plants and crops need the right amount of water—not too much and not too little—so growers may also track weather and rainfall to help determine whether and when to water their plants.

JUST FOR FUN Have you heard any good math jokes lately? How about these:

Q: Why is 6 afraid of 7?

A: Because 7 8 9!

Q: What did the 0 say to the 8?

A: Nice belt!

IT ADDS UP! You can wow your friends with this amazing math trick—the answer is always the same whatever numbers you use, so long as you follow these steps:

1. Take a three-digit number (the numbers must be in decreasing order) and invert it (write it backwards).

2. Subtract the inverted number from the original number.

3. Invert the answer. Now add that answer to its inverted version. The result will always be 1,089!

Example:

$$651 \rightarrow 156$$

$$651 - 156 = 495$$

$$495 \rightarrow 594$$

$$495 + 594 = 1,089$$

Fast Fact

If you add two even numbers, the sum will be an even number. And if you add two odd numbers, the sum will also be an even number. But if you add an odd and an even number, the sum will be an odd number.

CHAPTER 5

TRANSPORTATION

HOW does a hybrid car work?

The United States is a nation of automobiles. In fact, there are about 253 million of them on American roads. But cars have two big problems: they cause pollution and they run on gasoline, which is expensive. One solution that carmakers have come up with is the hybrid car. A hybrid car uses a combination of two power sources—gas and electricity.

Hybrid cars save on fuel. One way they do this is by running mostly on electricity provided by batteries. And because hybrids usually are smaller and lighter than regular cars, they need less power to run. Hybrid cars also don't pollute as much as cars that run on gasoline alone. Electricity doesn't give off any pollution, and hybrids burn less gas and do it more efficiently than gas-powered cars.

The batteries store electricity, which makes the electric motor run.

An electric motor powers the car. The motor also works as a generator to recharge the batteries.

The gas tank stores fuel that runs the gas engine. The tank holds less gas than those in regular cars.

The power electronics control how much electricity is used to run the car—and when to use it.

Many hybrid cars use special tires that are inflated more than usual. This causes less friction and saves on fuel.

The gas-powered engine runs the car at higher speeds or when the battery needs to be recharged. While this engine runs, it turns the generator.

Cars, trains, and planes make it a snap to travel just about anywhere. And new technologies promise that we'll be getting around faster and more efficiently than ever before.

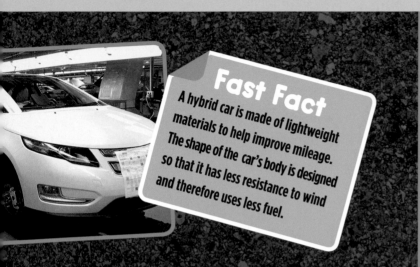

Fast Fact

A hybrid car is made of lightweight materials to help improve mileage. The shape of the car's body is designed so that it has less resistance to wind and therefore uses less fuel.

HYBRID VS. ELECTRIC

A hybrid car uses both an electric motor and a gas-powered engine. The hybrid uses the electric motor to travel at slow speeds. When the car goes at higher speeds, the gas engine turns on automatically. If more power is needed, the electric motor and gas engine can work at the same time. If the batteries run low, the gas engine will take over and recharge the batteries as the car runs.

A typical hybrid car battery is actually a battery pack, which is made up of individual cells working together. The number of cells varies, but a battery can contain more than 200 cells.

An electric car is powered only by electricity. It needs more batteries than a hybrid, often 12 to 24 of them. The batteries can last up to 250 miles before they need to be recharged.

SELF-DRIVING CARS

Self-driving cars rely on several key technologies. Conventional cars now have some of these features as well.

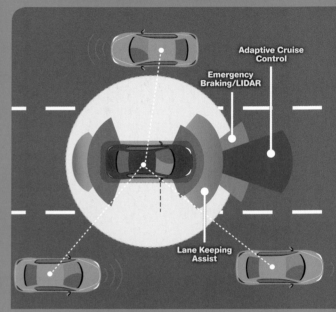

Adaptive Cruise Control

Emergency Braking/LIDAR

Lane Keeping Assist

Lane keeping assist technology uses cameras to detect lane markings on the road. If a driver drifts over the dividing line, an alert sounds. Some cars can steer themselves back on course.

Adaptive cruise control changes the car's speed to maintain a safe distance from the car ahead. The technology relies on a radar sensor to measure distance.

Self-braking systems use laser, radar, or video sensors to determine if objects are in the car's path. Brakes engage to slow or bring the car to a stop.

LIDAR (Light Detection and Ranging) maps a vehicle's environment in 3D. The best sensors spot details the size of a dime from more than 100 yards away. Self-driving cars are already on the road and may be a common sight within the next decade.

HOW does a maglev train work?

A levitating train floats in the air—but it's not a magic trick. *Maglev* is short for "magnetic levitation," and maglev trains use the push and pull of magnetism to travel above the tracks. The opposite poles of magnets attract each other. That attraction allows one kind of maglev train to levitate. Magnets surrounding the train cars attract the magnets on the train, pulling the entire train off the track. The same poles of magnets repel each other, which is why another kind of maglev train can float. Magnets on the tracks repel magnets on the train cars, pushing them up off the tracks. With no friction from wheels to slow them down, these magnetic marvels can reach speeds of more than 300 miles per hour.

Today, maglev trains are running full-time only in China, Japan, and South Korea and are being tested in other countries, including Germany. They may one day come to the United States. When that happens, people who love riding trains will really be floating on air!

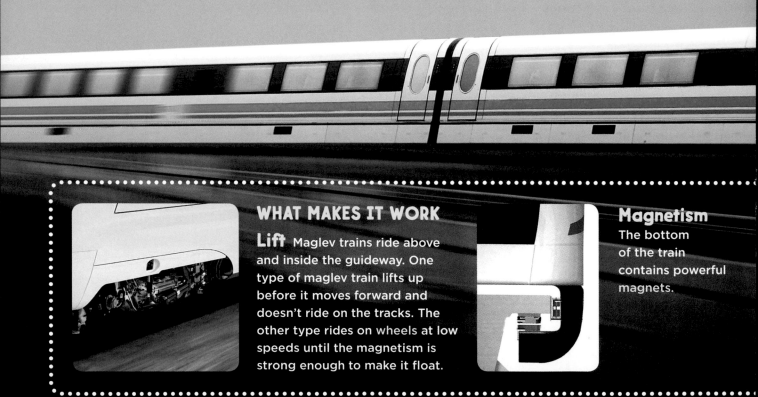

WHAT MAKES IT WORK

Lift Maglev trains ride above and inside the guideway. One type of maglev train lifts up before it moves forward and doesn't ride on the tracks. The other type rides on wheels at low speeds until the magnetism is strong enough to make it float.

Magnetism The bottom of the train contains powerful magnets.

TOP 5 FASTEST PASSENGER TRAINS

In 2015, a Japanese maglev train broke its own record on a test track, hitting 374 miles per hour. You can't ride that train yet, but here's how fast you'll go on the top five fastest passenger trains in the world.

TRAIN	OPERATING SPEED (MPH)	LOCATION
1. Shanghai Maglev Train	267	China
2. Harmony	236	China
3. AGV Italo	223	Italy
4. Renfe AVE	217	Spain
5. Deutsch Bahn ICE	205	Germany

Shanghai Maglev Train

AGV Italo

Renfe AVE

Electric Electricity sent through wires in the guideway creates an electromagnetic field. The magnetism attracts or repels the maglev's magnets (depending on the type of train), lifting the cars as much as three inches.

Motion Current in coils along the guideway constantly changes direction, reversing its magnetic field. The magnetism pulls the front of the train and pushes the back of the train. This makes the train go forward.

HOW does a helicopter take off and fly?

Helicopter flight seems like it would be impossible: a fragile-looking aircraft topped with spinning blades lifts straight into the air and travels swiftly in any direction. Yet a helicopter flies according to the same principles as an airplane.

Did You Know?

Helicopters are not easy to fly. Pilots must move multiple controls at the same time. The rate of accidents during pilot training is twice as high for helicopters as for airplanes. But these highly skilled pilots complete some of the most dangerous missions in the world—delivering soldiers and military supplies or accessing remote areas during rescue missions.

HANDS AND FEET The pilot uses both arms and legs to control the aircraft.

1 COLLECTIVE CONTROL This alters the pitch, or angle, of all of the blades equally and at the same time—that is, collectively. Increasing the pitch generates more lift, but also more drag, or wind resistance, so the pilot has to increase the engine power to keep the blades from slowing down.

2 THROTTLE This increases or decreases the speed.

3 CYCLIC PITCH STICK This directs the pitch of each blade individually, to move the helicopter forward, backward, or sideways.

4 ANTI-TORQUE PEDALS A pilot uses these to change the direction the nose is pointing.

5 YAW PEDALS Pedals at the pilot's feet change the pitch of the tail rotor, which turns the aircraft left or right.

LIFT

THRUST

DRAG

WEIGHT

1 All aircraft need lift to fly. Lift is the force that opposes the weight of the craft and keeps it in the air. Helicopter blades, called airfoils, are curved on top and flat on the bottom—just like airplane wings. This shape causes air to move faster over the tops of the blades than under the bottoms. On a small helicopter, the main rotor will make almost 500 revolutions per minute (rpm), whipping the tips of the blades at near-supersonic speed. The air movement over the blades creates low pressure above them and high pressure below, causing enough lift to overcome the weight of the aircraft.

2 As the blades spin, Newton's third law of motion kicks in. This law says that for every movement there is an equal movement in the opposite direction. The body of a helicopter wants to spin in the direction opposite to the direction of the blades. To solve this problem, a coaxial rotor on the rotor mast spins in the opposite direction, to cancel out the torque, or turning force, of the main rotor.

HOW are tunnels dug?

Tunnels are dug through miles of mountains or under cities to make passageways for trains and cars. A mammoth piece of equipment called a tunnel-boring machine (TBM) is used to dig the huge holes. It has a giant spinning disk that cuts through solid rock. TBMs were used to cut through mountains of the Alps to create the longest tunnel ever built—the Gotthard Base Tunnel, which is in Europe, and links Switzerland and Italy. The train tunnel is slightly more than 35 miles long!

Sometimes when transportation tunnels are dug, two tunnels are built side by side so cars or trains can travel in both directions. Most tunnels are dug from the opposite ends and meet in the middle.

The TBMs for the Gotthard tunnel each weighed about 6 million pounds and were 1,300 feet long. They dug 96 feet of tunnel a week. It takes 20 to 25 people to operate a TBM.

TOP 5 LONGEST RAILROAD TUNNELS

TUNNEL	LOCATION	LENGTH (MILES)	OPENED
1. Gotthard Base	Switzerland	35.4	2016
2. Seikan	Japan	33.5	1988
3. Yulhyeon	South Korea	32.5	2016
4. Channel	Britain-France	31.1	1994
5. Songshan Lake	China	24.1	2016

4 An elevator carries dug-up rock to the surface. The rock might be placed in a landfill or used in another project, such as a road. At Gotthard, some rock was used to make the concrete that lines the tunnel walls.

Surface

1 The rotating cutters of the TBM can be 50 feet in diameter. Their superstrong titanium teeth rotate slowly, breaking up the rock as the TBM moves forward.

3 A conveyor belt carries crumbled rock to the back of the TBM. The rock drops into a cart and is removed from the area.

Concrete sections to line the tunnel are lowered down a shaft.

5 The walls of a finished tunnel are usually lined with steel or concrete or a combination of both materials. The Gotthard tunnel walls are made of concrete and a special steel that won't break under the great pressure of the Alps.

2 The front of some TBMs have shields to keep pieces of rock from falling down and burying the machine.

Fast Fact
The Gotthard tunnel took more than 17 years and 2,400 workers to build. Temperatures in the tunnel during construction reached 122° F.

HOW does a 120,000-ton cruise ship float?

Currently, the world's largest cruise ship is Royal Caribbean's *Harmony of the Seas*. It stretches 1,188 feet, or almost four football fields, in length. Its beam, or width at the widest point, measures 154 feet. It weighs 120,000 tons. Yet it floats according to the same principles as a little rowboat. Any boat's seaworthiness depends on buoyancy, water displacement, materials, and design.

HARMONY OF THE SEAS BY THE NUMBERS

Passengers: 6,780 guests and 2,100 crew

Decks: 18 (16 for passengers and two for crew)

Elevators: 24

Eggs used per day: 500 dozen

Chocolate ice cream served per day: 100 gallons

MATERIALS AND DESIGN To achieve buoyancy, a ship must be made of sturdy, lightweight materials that are denser than water, such as extra-strong steel. The wide, U-shaped design of a cruise ship's hull helps disperse the ship's weight across its body. This design also helps push water aside for a smooth, straight ride.

As protection in the event of a collision—with, say, an iceberg—shipbuilders construct a ship with a double hull, one hull inside the other. Bulkheads, or watertight dividers, can be closed to keep water from rushing through a damaged hull.

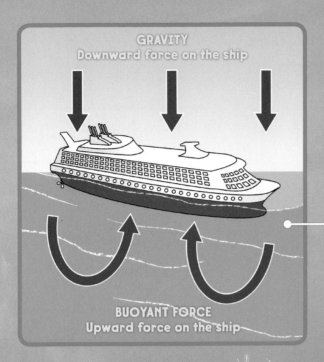

GRAVITY
Downward force on the ship

BUOYANT FORCE
Upward force on the ship

BUOYANCY AND DISPLACEMENT When a ship is in the water, it displaces, or moves aside, the water beneath it. For a ship to float, it cannot weigh more than the water it displaces. The upward buoyant force is equal to the weight of the water being displaced. The weight of the water displaced by *Harmony of the Seas* is 120,000 tons. That means the weight of the ship is also 120,000 tons. This way of calculating a ship's weight was devised by Greek scientist Archimedes in around 250 B.C. (more than 2,000 years ago).

The tugboat gives a water spray sendoff as the cruise ship sets out to sea. This traditional custom celebrates the arrival or departure of a vessel.

ROUGH SEAS When waves tilt a ship from side to side, it's called rolling—which tends to make passengers seasick. To stabilize a large cruise ship, engineers make the hull extremely wide. Stabilizing fins below the water also limit a ship's roll. If a ship begins to list, or lean, to one side, the ship's crew will pump water from one side to the other to balance the ship.

But the extreme height of these ships—243 feet for *Harmony of the Seas*—puts them at risk of wind damage during hurricanes. So how do large ships handle hurricane conditions? They avoid them! Crews monitor weather conditions and wind directions and move to calmer waters when storms approach.

HOW TO
make a paper airplane

People have been making objects out of paper for centuries. In Japan, the art of folding paper is called origami (or-eh-*gahm*-ee). An origami expert can make almost anything out of a piece of paper—from a hang glider to a beetle to a race car. Here's how you can fold a sheet of paper into an airplane that flies. It's an uplifting experience!

What you need:

• A sheet of paper 8 1/2 inches by 11 inches. The paper can be smaller or bigger, but it should be rectangular.

ODD LOOKING Something's missing from this teardrop-shaped Martin Marietta X-24 plane—wings! The U.S. Air Force built it to test how a spacecraft might act when reentering Earth's atmosphere. Even wingless, it went 1,036 miles per hour.

What to do:

1 Take a sheet of paper and fold it in half the long way. Then open the paper so there is a crease down the middle.

2 Fold in one corner so that it lines up with the center crease. Do the same with the corner across from it.

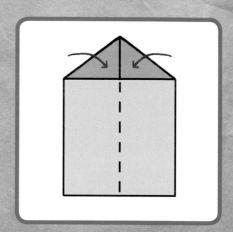

3 Fold each outer corner so it lines up with the center crease.

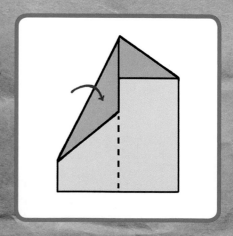

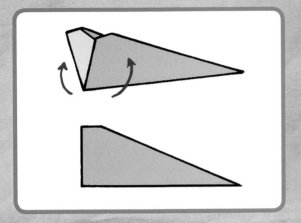

④ Fold along the main crease so you can see the body of the airplane.

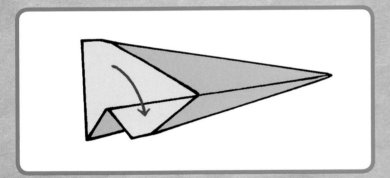

⑤ Fold one wing down so its edge lines up with the center crease. Repeat with the other wing.

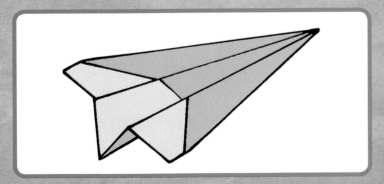

⑥ Unfold the wings so your plane is ready for takeoff. Throw it like a dart to make it fly. If it crashes too quickly, adjust the wings.

SPEEDSTERS

In 2004, NASA's X-43A set the speed record as the fastest jet-powered aircraft. For 10 seconds, the unpiloted test craft traveled at Mach 9.6, or more than nine times the speed of sound. That's 7,000 miles per hour!

The fastest piloted aircraft is the North American X-15. In October 1967, Air Force Major William "Pete" Knight broke all records, hitting 4,520 miles per hour, or Mach 6.72.

PRO TIP According to Takuo Toda, an engineer and chair of the Japan Origami Airplane Association, the best way to keep a paper airplane aloft is to throw it straight up in the air.

CHAPTER 6

HOME TECH

HOW does a toilet flush away waste?

Getting rid of poop can be a problem. The earliest form of waste disposal was a pit in the ground. In ancient India, some cities had toilets that drained waste into underground chambers. The toilets of early Romans dropped waste into running water that carried it away. During the Middle Ages, many people in Europe deposited their waste in bowls, called chamber pots. People sometimes threw the contents out the window and into the street, where it flowed into open drains.

It wasn't until 1596 that Englishman John Harington invented the first flush toilet. Over the following centuries, advances were made in toilet technology—as well as in toilet-related products. For example, in 1857, Joseph Gayetty came up with the idea of selling toilet paper in a package. The Scott Paper Company started selling toilet paper on a roll in 1879.

By the early 1900s, the modern toilet had been developed. Instead of the flap system shown here, some modern toilets are designed with canister valves. The toilet may now be the most important seat in the house.

1 When the handle is pressed, a chain lifts a flap.

2 The flap covers a hole at the bottom of the tank. When the flap lifts up, all the water in the tank pours into the bowl. When the tank is empty, the flap closes.

The tank can hold several gallons of water.

3 After the bowl fills with water, the siphon sucks everything into a pipe that leads to the sewer system.

Did You Know?

Among the many names for toilet are latrine, water closet, privy, lavatory, throne, chamber pot, commode, and john.

Your home has plenty of incredible inventions that you probably take for granted. In this chapter, you'll discover many machines that make life easier.

4 As the tank empties, the float sinks. When the float reaches the bottom of the tank, it opens a valve, sending water into the tank. As the tank fills, the float rises. At the top of the tank, the float shuts the valve, cutting off the water. Now you can flush again.

Fast Fact

Yikes! Before toilet paper came along, people used a scary variety of items to clean up after visits to the toilet. Outhouses often had old store catalogs hanging in them, and the pages were put to good use as a rough kind of toilet paper. Earlier "goers" used sponges, moss, corncobs, or even clay. We can all be thankful for modern conveniences.

WASTE NOT...

Most toilets whoosh down several gallons of water every time they flush. Toilets account for 25% of all water used in a house. To save water, new types of toilets have been invented.

Modern toilets

A modern toilet is able to flush using only 1.6 gallons of water. Old toilets used between three and five gallons a flush. That can save the average home 100 gallons a day.

Dual-flush toilets

A dual-flush toilet allows the user to flush two different ways. Press one button for solid waste, and the toilet uses 1.6 gallons. For liquid waste, it flushes only 0.79 gallons.

Composting toilets

A composting toilet uses almost no water. The waste goes into a container that changes it into compost, which is used to fertilize the soil. Compost is made when bacteria break down natural substances. The owner of a composting toilet might have to add air, worms, or bacteria to the container to help the waste become safe compost. Fans remove any smells in the bathroom through a pipe that leads outside.

HOW can you make your house greener?

Going green means trying to reduce pollution and preserve natural resources. People can go green at school, at work, and especially at home. Many factors make a building green—from the materials used in its construction to the placement of the windows. One way to make a building green is to build it with materials that don't harm the people inside it or the environment. Another way is to make sure the building doesn't use a lot of energy for heating or cooling. Eco-friendly buildings are often powered by sustainable resources such as sunlight. Green builders also try to recycle and reuse materials during construction.

Going green can save money on energy bills and be better for the health of people—and the health of the planet. Check out some ways to make a home more friendly to the environment.

1. Solar panels on the roof can generate electricity from sunlight.

2. Plants in the house can remove pollutants from the air. Rubber plants, Boston ferns, and palm trees work well.

3. Lower the temperature on your thermostat by a few degrees in the winter, and raise it by a few in the summer. This saves energy.

4. Floors and furniture can be made from reused wood, which is wood recycled from old buildings or discarded furniture. Use wood, such as bamboo, that doesn't come from endangered forests.

5. Use cloth towels and napkins instead of ones made of paper.

6. Use low-flow faucets in the kitchen and bathroom. They reduce the amount of water used for washing and showering.

7. Replace regular incandescent light bulbs with LED lightbulbs, which use 75% less energy, and last 25 times longer.

8. Low-flow toilets use 20% less water per flush.

9. Computers and other electronics use power even when they're turned off. Unplug them when not in use, or connect them to a power strip that you can turn off to stop the drain of electricity.

10. Plant shade trees and put up awnings or shades to keep sunlight from making the house too warm. Inside, cool off with fans instead of air-conditioners.

11. To reduce energy use, insulate the walls to keep heat and cold from escaping outside.

12. Fill in the openings around doors and windows to keep out the weather.

13. All new appliances should have an Energy Star label on them, especially the fridge, which uses a great amount of energy. Products with these labels use less electricity than older models.

HOW does a microwave oven cook food?

There's fast food. And there's faster food. A microwave oven heats some foods in a minute or less. A microwave oven cooks with a type of radiation called microwaves, which are similar to the waves that transmit Wi-Fi. Microwaves don't heat air. Instead, they penetrate food, making the food's water and fat molecules vibrate. The vibrations produce heat in a jiffy. Because microwaves don't heat most plastic, ceramics, paper, or glass, food is often microwaved on dishes made of these materials. When you take a cool plate from a microwave, you may be fooled into thinking the food isn't hot. But it is—so be careful before you take a bite!

2 Microwaves bounce off a kind of fan called a stirrer. This scatters the microwaves throughout the oven. The microwaves bounce around until they enter the food.

1 Electricity passes through a tube called a magnetron, which produces microwaves. This energy is aimed at the stirrer.

3 Microwaves cause water in the food to vibrate more than 2 billion times a second. This vibration causes friction, which produces energy in the form of heat. Food won't cook unless it is in—or contains—some water.

4 A turntable spins so the microwaves reach all parts of the food.

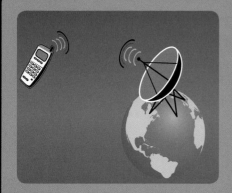

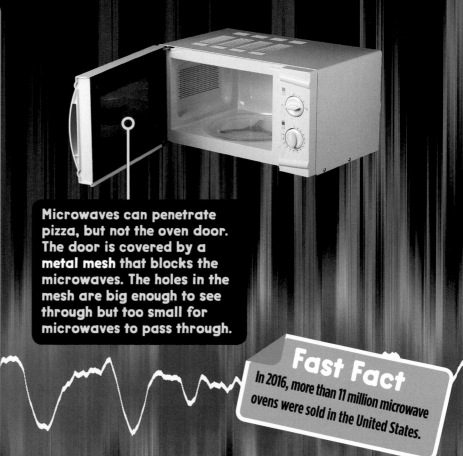

When you make a cell phone call, you're using the same kind of energy you use to make microwave popcorn. Most cell phone calls are transmitted by microwaves, which also connect Earth with satellites. This handy energy is very versatile: it's used in medicine to treat certain skin diseases and types of cancer, and in industry to reduce air pollutants and disinfect hospital waste.

Microwaves can penetrate pizza, but not the oven door. The door is covered by a **metal mesh** that blocks the microwaves. The holes in the mesh are big enough to see through but too small for microwaves to pass through.

Fast Fact

In 2016, more than 11 million microwave ovens were sold in the United States.

MICROWAVE MAN

In 1946, Percy Spencer was testing a device called a magnetron in a lab when he discovered something strange. A candy bar in his pocket had melted. Spencer put some unpopped popcorn near the magnetron. Pretty soon, the popcorn started popping. Spencer realized that microwaves produced by the magnetron could cook food. Spencer and the company he worked for eventually built a microwave oven. It was more than five feet high and two feet wide and weighed 670 pounds. Only commercial kitchens had space for ovens that huge. It wasn't until about 20 years later that a smaller, home version of the microwave oven was introduced. It soon became a popular cooking tool in people's kitchens.

HOW does a lock work?

There are locks for bikes, locks for bank vaults, locks for doors and windows, locks for diaries, and locks for lockers. Just about everyone keeps valuables under lock and key. People have been doing that since the time of the ancient Egyptians, who made large wooden locks and keys about 4,000 years ago. The ancient Romans and Chinese built simple locks from metal.

Locks didn't change much until the end of the 1700s, when a few Englishmen began to make devices more secure. Today, a variety of locks keep items safe, from combination locks with numbered dials, to vaults that use timing devices, to locks that operate with magnetic keys.

One of the most common locks used today is a cylinder with pins inside. To open it, a key with the right shape lifts the pins. This is called a pin and tumbler lock.

A PIN AND TUMBLER LOCK

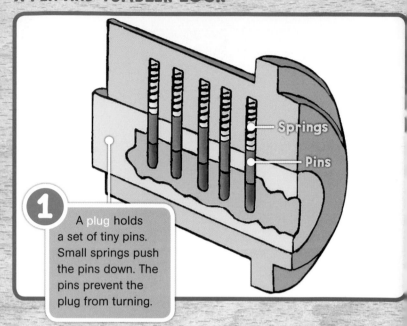

Springs

Pins

1 A plug holds a set of tiny pins. Small springs push the pins down. The pins prevent the plug from turning.

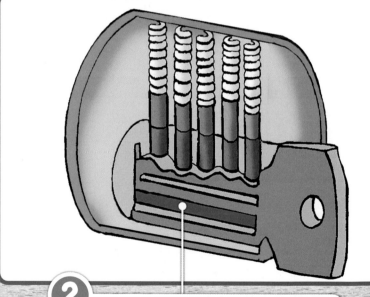

2 The key slides into the plug. If the key has edges with the correct shape, it will push up the pins until they are out of the way. Now the key can turn the plug. A key with the wrong-shaped edges won't lift all the pins out of the way, and the key won't turn.

Fast Fact

In 1948, Linus Yale, Sr. patented a pin and tumbler lock that fit in a cylinder. His son, Linus, Jr., improved the lock, which today is called a Yale lock.

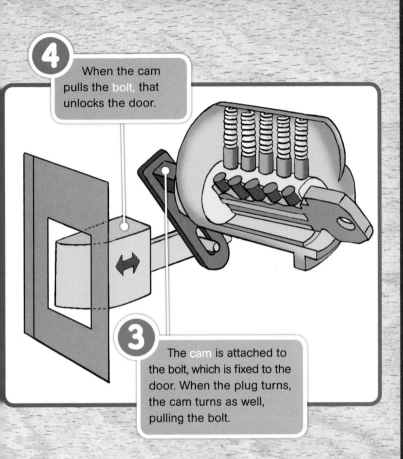

4 When the cam pulls the bolt, that unlocks the door.

3 The cam is attached to the bolt, which is fixed to the door. When the plug turns, the cam turns as well, pulling the bolt.

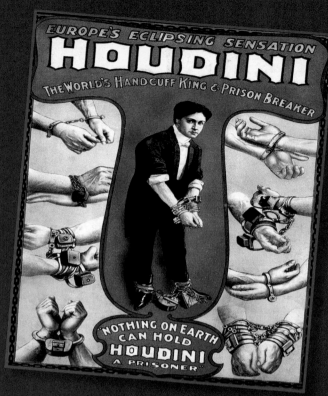

Did You Know?

Not all doors have keyholes. Many hotels and office buildings use locks that open with plastic cards. Each card has a magnetic strip on the back and magnets in a lock read that strip. If it contains the right information—the correct room number, for example—the magnets trigger the lock to open. If it has the wrong info— sorry, you're locked out!

LOCK AND ROLL

Not many locks could hold Harry Houdini, who lived from 1874 to 1926. The world's most famous escape artist, Houdini would let himself be locked up in ways that made escape seem impossible. Yet he always broke free. In the early 1900s, Houdini challenged police in many cities to chain and handcuff him and lock him in the local jail. Each time, Houdini escaped. He freed himself from many other hair-raising situations, such as a locked crate thrown into a river and a locked glass container filled with water.

How did he do it? Houdini knew how to pick, or open, just about any type of lock. He was able to open handcuffs by banging them against hard surfaces. He could open a lock with a shoelace. Houdini also cheated: He hid tools for opening locks, as well as keys. When he couldn't hide a key, he swallowed it and brought it up when no one was looking. If his hands were bound, he could turn the key with his teeth!

HOW does a zipper zip?

How could we live without zippers? Well, people managed to survive without them for thousands of years. In ancient times, people held together their animal-hide clothes with pins made of thorns. Later civilizations, such as the Greeks and Egyptians, kept clothes from opening with metal pins and clasps, or cloth ties. A major fastener advance came in the Middle Ages with the invention of the button (and the buttonhole, of course). In the 1800s, two more improvements were introduced: safety pins and snaps.

The big fastener breakthrough came from Gideon Sundback. He invented the modern zipper in 1913. Still, this fastener didn't catch on until the 1930s, when it got the name *zipper*. Suddenly, zippers were sewn onto just about anything that opened and closed, from dresses to rubber boots. Today, YKK, a company that has its U.S. headquarters in Georgia, makes almost half the zippers in the world. Is the zipper an important invention? Look in your closet: it's an open-and-shut case!

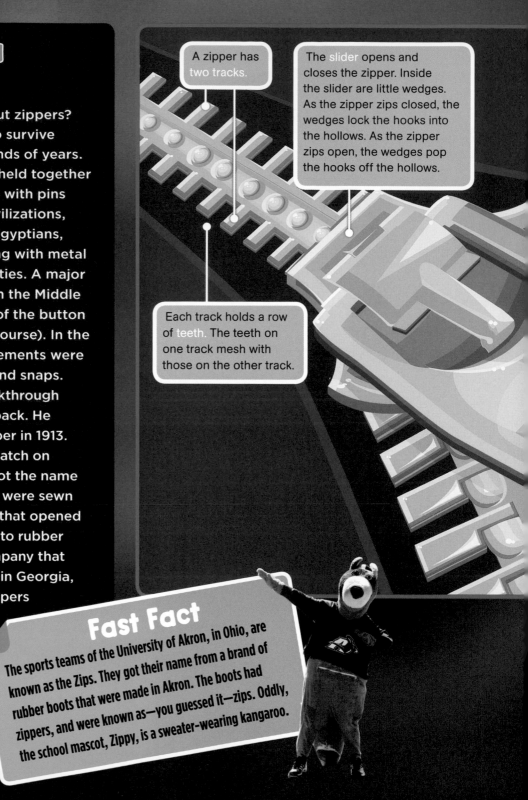

A zipper has two tracks.

The slider opens and closes the zipper. Inside the slider are little wedges. As the zipper zips closed, the wedges lock the hooks into the hollows. As the zipper zips open, the wedges pop the hooks off the hollows.

Each track holds a row of teeth. The teeth on one track mesh with those on the other track.

Fast Fact

The sports teams of the University of Akron, in Ohio, are known as the Zips. They got their name from a brand of rubber boots that were made in Akron. The boots had zippers, and were known as—you guessed it—zips. Oddly, the school mascot, Zippy, is a sweater-wearing kangaroo.

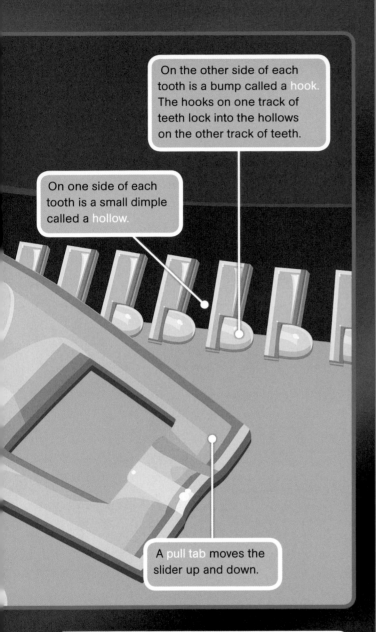

On the other side of each tooth is a bump called a hook. The hooks on one track of teeth lock into the hollows on the other track of teeth.

On one side of each tooth is a small dimple called a hollow.

A pull tab moves the slider up and down.

Did You Know?

The word *zipper* is an example of onomatopoeia (on-oh-mah-toh-*pee*-ah). An onomatopoeic word's sound suggests its meaning. *Zipper* sounds like the noise a zipper makes. A few other such words are *splat, buzz, snort, honk, tinkle, beep, crash, sizzle, slurp,* and *whir.* Can you think of other examples of onomatopoeia?

FASTEN-ATING INVENTION

Instead of using zippers, some clothes and other items are fastened with Velcro®, which was the brainchild of Swiss engineer George de Mestral. In 1948, after taking his dogs out for a walk in the woods, he noticed burrs sticking to the animals' fur. De Mestral thought those clingy seedpods from the burdock plant might have a use.

After seven years of testing, de Mestral invented a fastener based on the burr. It came in two parts: a cotton strip covered with tiny hooks, and a cotton strip covered with tiny loops. The two strips stuck together. De Mestral called his invention Velcro, a combination of the words *velvet* and *crochet.* (Crochet is a kind of knitting.) Later, nylon replaced cotton, and Velcro became the new zipper.

Today, this fastener is used on everything from hospital gowns, airplane seat cushions, and diapers to car floor mats, carpets, and sneakers. NASA attaches Velcro to objects to keep them from floating around in space. Some Velcro is so strong that a five-inch-square piece can hold a one-ton load. Velcro is a perfect invention except for one thing . . . that ripping sound!

To NOD

HOW does a refrigerator keep food cold?

Food needs to chill out. When the temperature is above 40°F, bacteria can grow in food and spoil it. Refrigerators keep food cool so it doesn't go bad. What did people do before they had modern fridges? They packed food in snow and ice, put it underwater, or placed it in cool cellars.

The cooling system of a fridge is more complicated. Refrigerators contain a chemical coolant. As this chemical passes through the fridge's pipes, it changes from a liquid to a gas to a liquid, over and over. The refrigerant becomes a gas at very low temperatures. As the liquid refrigerant circulates through the inside of the fridge, heat makes the liquid evaporate, or turn into gas. The gas absorbs heat, making everything in the fridge cold. This is also what happens when you sweat on a warm day. As the sweat evaporates, your skin chills. Cool!

1 Refrigerant in the form of gas travels into a compressor, which is powered by an electric motor. The compressor squeezes the gas and pushes it through the fridge's pipes. As the gas is squeezed, it heats up.

2 The compressor sends the hot gas through condensers, which are coils of tubes outside the fridge. The outside air cools the gas. As it cools, the gas condenses, or turns into liquid.

Did You Know?

Freezers work in much the same way as refrigerators—the big difference is the speed of the refrigerant (see step 1). In a freezer's coils, the gas moves very quickly, making the freezer colder than the fridge. And there you have it . . . ice cubes and frozen peas!

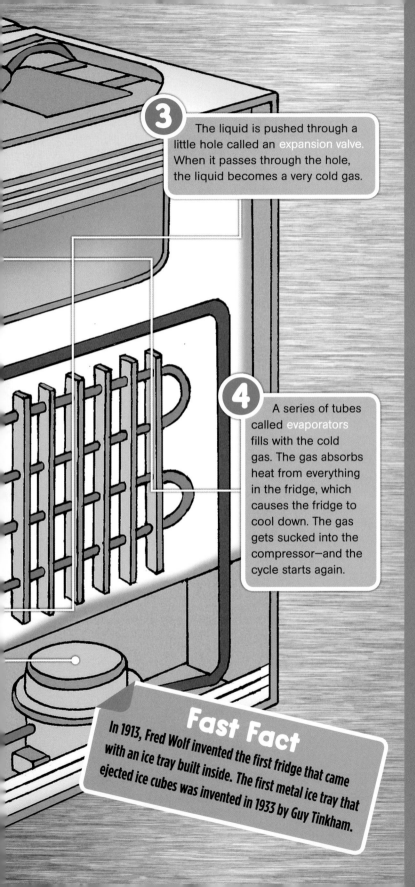

③ The liquid is pushed through a little hole called an expansion valve. When it passes through the hole, the liquid becomes a very cold gas.

④ A series of tubes called evaporators fills with the cold gas. The gas absorbs heat from everything in the fridge, which causes the fridge to cool down. The gas gets sucked into the compressor—and the cycle starts again.

Fast Fact

In 1913, Fred Wolf invented the first fridge that came with an ice tray built inside. The first metal ice tray that ejected ice cubes was invented in 1933 by Guy Tinkham.

CHILLIN'

Most freezers in home refrigerators go down to 0°F, which keeps ice cream nice and firm. But there are colder places than freezers. Check out the lowest of the low.

On an average day, the temperature in the Arctic is about -30°F. The coldest temperature recorded in the Arctic was -89°F. Kids bundle up for school recess.

Antarctica is the world's coldest place, with winter temperatures reaching -94°F. The coldest temperature ever recorded on Earth was reported here: -128.6°F.

Some of the coldest places in the universe are inside cosmic clouds. These clouds of gas and dust are far from stars, and dust blocks any radiation that reaches them. The temperature inside one might be as cold as -425°F. The coldest anything in the universe can get is -460°F. That's called absolute zero.

HOW TO make a camera obscura

Remember to ask an adult for help.

The oldest and cheapest camera ever made is the camera obscura. *Camera obscura* means "dark chamber," which describes this simple device. A camera obscura is a dark room with a small hole in one wall. Light reflects off an object outside the wall. The light passes through the hole and makes an upside-down image of the object on the opposite wall. The image is very clear because a tiny hole focuses light. If the hole were large, the light hitting the wall would scatter and make the image of the object look blurry.

A camera obscura can show only what is directly outside the room. To view something else, you'd have to carry the room around. This isn't very practical, so people learned how to make portable versions of the device. Here's how you can make one, too.

What you need:

- Ruler
- Empty cylindrical can with a metal bottom, such as a potato chip can
- Marker, pen, or pencil
- Utility knife (for an adult to use)
- Thumbtack or pushpin
- Wax paper or white tissue paper
- Scissors
- Masking or electrical tape
- Aluminum foil

What to do:

1 With the ruler, measure two inches from the bottom of the can. Draw lines around the can at that point. Have an adult cut the can into two pieces along the line.

2 Use the thumbtack or pushpin to make a tiny hole in the center of the metal bottom of the can. Spin the tack in the hole to smooth the sides of the hole.

3 Cut out a circle of wax paper or tissue paper. Stretch it as tightly as possible over the open top of the short part of the can and tape it into place.

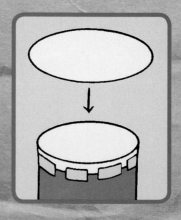

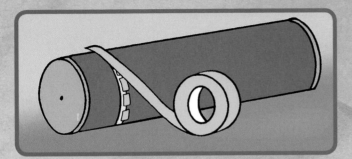

4 Place the long part of the can next to the short part. Tape the two parts of the can together so it looks like it did before you cut it.

6 Place an object under bright light, point the pinhole at it, and look through the opening. Place your hands around the opening to keep out light. You should see the object on the wax paper, but upside down. Move your camera closer or farther away until the object is in focus.

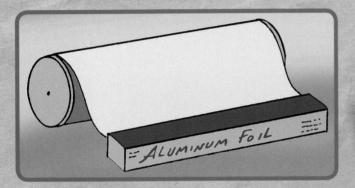

5 Wrap aluminum foil around the can, lining up the edges with the top and bottom of the can. If there is extra foil at the top, fold it into the can. Make sure no light enters the can except through the hole in the bottom and the opening at the top.

CAMERA OBSCURA This illustration from the 1500s shows the image of a solar eclipse projected into a darkened room through a small hole (the image is inverted).

CELL PHONE CAMERA TIPS

Today, most cell phones have cameras. Here's a how-to for using them to take the best pictures you can.

✳ Keep the lens clean. Use a soft cloth (not your finger) to wipe it.

✳ Don't use the zoom function to take faraway shots. Move as close as you can to your subject, then use the zoom during editing and cropping.

✳ Steady does it! Put the phone on a solid surface or hold it with both hands when taking a picture.

✳ Avoid cluttered or busy backgrounds behind your subjects.

✳ Have fun! Try different angles and points of view.

CHAPTER 7

TECHNOLOGY

HOW does a 3D printer make objects?

The first step in 3D printing is to make a blueprint of the object using special computer-aided design (CAD) software. There is no limit to what designers can draft—sneakers, instruments, and even cars have been made using 3D printing technology. After the blueprints are final, it's time to get started.

How does it work? Instead of shooting ink onto paper, a 3D printer shoots thin layers of plastic that gradually form objects. Material jetting, in which the printer emits material straight from a nozzle, is one technology used in 3D printing. Binder jetting is another. In binder jetting, the printer sprays a gluelike substance over a thin layer of powder, causing the powder to stick together, or bind. The printer deposits new layers of powder, eventually producing an object.

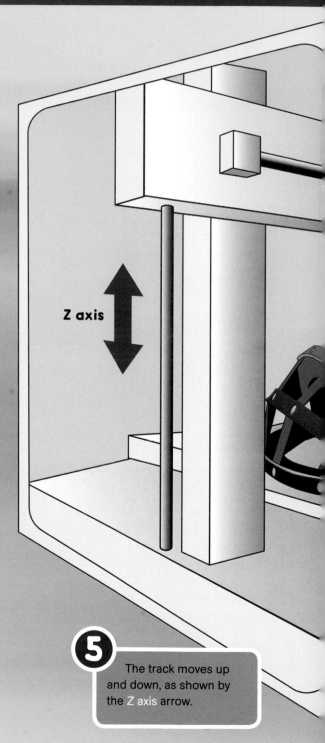

Z axis

When New York–based designer Christian Von Heifner created the prototype for his foldable FEND bike helmet, he used a 3D printer. The helmet can be tucked into a bag or pocket between rides.

5 The track moves up and down, as shown by the Z axis arrow.

Technology affects almost every aspect of our lives, and it's changing all the time. Learn how people connect via social media, how smartphones are made, and just how cool 3D printers are.

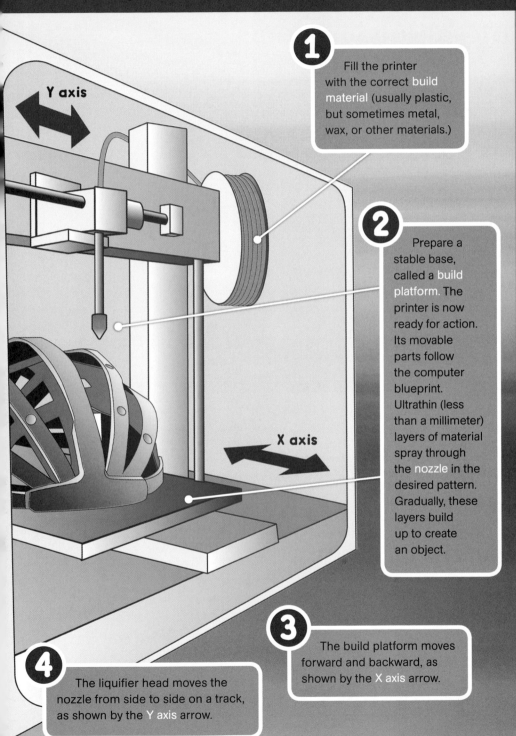

Y axis

X axis

1 Fill the printer with the correct build material (usually plastic, but sometimes metal, wax, or other materials.)

2 Prepare a stable base, called a build platform. The printer is now ready for action. Its movable parts follow the computer blueprint. Ultrathin (less than a millimeter) layers of material spray through the nozzle in the desired pattern. Gradually, these layers build up to create an object.

3 The build platform moves forward and backward, as shown by the X axis arrow.

4 The liquifier head moves the nozzle from side to side on a track, as shown by the Y axis arrow.

ONE AT A TIME

3D printing could change the way products are manufactured. Instead of factories making huge quantities of goods, people will be able to print products individually as they need them, even tailoring items to their own specifications and designs.

3D printed shoes

PRINTING FOOD

In 2014, a Spanish company unveiled the Foodini, a 3D printer that creates meals out of edible ingredients. The Foodini makes everything from intricately designed foods like cake decorations to time-consuming recipes such as stuffed ravioli. Its inventors wanted to design an appliance that would make home cooking easier.

3D printed food

HOW does social media connect people all around the world?

Facebook. Twitter. Instagram. Snapchat. These social media platforms may look different on a computer or smartphone screen, but they all have one thing in common: they enable people around the world to communicate almost instantly. How do they do it? Through a combination of high-tech computer programming and data storage devices called servers. When users interact with these sites, they provide information—such as messages or photos sent to friends—that the websites gather and store on giant servers. Social media programmers write code that manipulates the data in different ways—for instance, by recommending new social connections based on current networks of people. Social media platforms set minimum ages—in most cases, users must be 13 or older.

TOP SITE As of 2017, Facebook had the most active users of any social media site, with 1.9 billion users. Next is WhatsApp (1.2 billion), followed by YouTube (1 billion) and Facebook Messenger (1 billion). Farther down the list are Instagram (600 million), Twitter (319 million), and Snapchat (300 million). You can use the graph below to compare the number of users for some top social media platforms. Each figure represents 100 million users.

Facebook

WhatsApp

YouTube

Twitter

Snapchat

Pyramid in Egypt

BIG AND BIGGER How many users a social media platform has and how much data the company stores factor into the number of servers needed. Some companies have special server rooms with rows of cabinets that hold dozens of servers each. Others fill entire buildings. Individual server units slip into slots in the cabinets. Each individual server unit contains many components, including one or more processors, memory, and power supply.

Eiffel Tower in France

Fast Fact

When you post an image or comment on social media, it exists forever—at least in the digital world—so potential employers, school admissions officers, and others can see it, even years later. Remember: if you don't want to share a photo or information with the whole world, don't post it!

DATA STORAGE A server is a separate computer that your computer, smartphone, or tablet accesses when you're surfing the web or using social media. When you post information to a social media site, you communicate with a database stored on a server. The server then sends this information out to your social network. A site like Facebook, which has nearly 2 billion registered users, needs so many servers to process data that the company maintains its own server farm, above, in Oregon.

Lincoln Memorial in the United States

HOW does Wi-Fi connect to the Internet?

A hot spot sounds like a place to avoid. But not if you're a Wi-Fi user. A hotspot is an area where a computer can connect to the Internet without being plugged in to electrical, telephone, or cable lines. Wi-Fi uses radio waves to link computers to other computers or to an Internet service. Wi-Fi works almost anywhere. It lets a person go online while moving from room to room. Users can also connect to the Internet in a coffee shop, a library, a schoolroom, a hotel, an airport, or even an airplane thousands of feet in the air. On a plane, the Wi-Fi signal may be linked to a satellite, to towers on the ground, or both.

Almost all new laptops and many new desktop computers are set up for wireless use. If a computer doesn't come with wireless, a wireless adapter can be added to it. It may also need a special software program to connect to a wireless network.

1 To connect to the Internet, an adapter in the computer changes digital data into a radio signal. The radio signal is similar to those used to broadcast radio and TV shows. An antenna inside the computer transmits the radio signal to a device called a router.

2 A router is an electronic device that joins together several computer networks, either through a wire or wirelessly. It contains an antenna, which receives the signal that the computer sends. A router works best when it is placed near a computer and away from objects that might block its signal, such as walls or furniture. The router translates the information from the computer and sends it to a modem.

WORLDWIDE WI-FI

Cities around the world are installing municipal wireless networks that provide Internet access to residents and visitors. Multiple Wi-Fi access points are arranged to interact with each other over a wide area. In some cities, a small access fee is charged, but in many places, the network is free. Cities with robust municipal wireless networks include New York City; Tel Aviv, Israel; Osaka, Japan; Perth, Australia; and Barcelona, Spain.

GOING WIRELESS The only thing that is possibly better than a wireless computer is a wireless video game. In 2002, Nintendo introduced the WaveBird controller for its GameCube, the first popular console that had a wireless remote control. In 2006, Nintendo introduced the Wii. As a player moves the wireless controller, the figure on the screen moves as well. PlayStation Move for PS3 also has a wireless wand, or controller. A camera on the console tracks the wand's movements.

In 2010, Xbox 360 introduced Kinect. Kinect isn't just wireless—it drops the controller altogether. It uses an infrared camera that instantly tracks the movements of the player's body and hands. When the player moves, the figure on the screen moves the same way. The virtual reality (VR) headset is one of the latest innovations in gaming. Oculus Rift and Samsung Gear VR are examples of VR technology. Users with headsets feel like they are experiencing gaming action directly. They can also watch movies, television, and sports coverage on VR systems.

3 The modem links a computer to the Internet. It changes the digital information in the computer to a form that can be sent through phone or cable television lines. The signal goes to servers that change it back into a digital form. These servers are joined to form a network— the Internet. To receive Internet through Wi-Fi, the process works in reverse. A signal goes from the Internet, to a modem, to a router, and then to a computer.

4 For Wi-Fi to work properly, a computer should be no more than about 120 feet from a router. Outdoors, the maximum distance is around 300 feet. This allows people to use Wi-Fi outdoors in public spaces like parks, as well as in cafés and restaurants with hot spots.

HOW can a virus make your computer sick?

Just like people, computers can get sick from viruses. Computer viruses work a little like viruses that infect humans. They spread by making copies of themselves. Once inside a computer, a virus can harm it in different ways, such as by making the computer run slowly or crash often, or by erasing the hard drive. Computer viruses are made and sent out by people who want to make trouble.

Computer viruses first began appearing in the late 1980s. That's when the personal computer boom began. Computer users started downloading programs and exchanging data disks. That made the spread of viruses simple. Today, there are "cures" for computer viruses, and so virus creators must constantly find new ways to infect computers. It's important for computer users to know the causes and symptoms of viruses.

WORM This software program can copy itself from one computer to another without attaching itself to other programs. Worms can avoid security blocks and quickly spread from one computer to every computer in a network, such as a company or government organization. Worms also spread through e-mail address books. Worms can destroy files, and slow down or stop programs from working.

SOFTWARE VIRUS This is a small bit of software that gets into a computer and secretly attaches itself to other programs. Every time a user opens a program, the virus also opens and starts to run. It can reproduce itself by latching onto other programs. The virus program interferes with the workings of the computer, damages files, or causes annoying messages to appear on the screen. It does not normally target hardware—the physical parts of the computer—although sometimes it does.

TROJAN VIRUS In this ancient story, Greek soldiers hid inside a giant wooden horse that was presented as a gift to the people of Troy. When the Trojans brought the horse into their city, the Greeks got out and attacked. In the same way, a Trojan virus will pretend to be music, a video, or some other desirable program. But when the program is downloaded, the virus attacks the computer. This virus can erase a hard drive, force the computer to show ads, or allow a hacker to gain partial control of the computer.

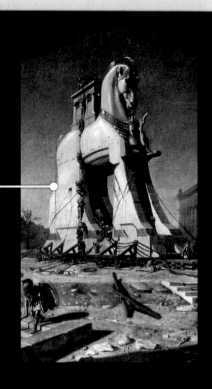

From:

Subject:

Date: January 10, 2017 6:59:26 AM PST

To:

▶ 📎 1 Attachment, 3.5 MB (Save ▾)

Good Morning!

E-MAIL VIRUS This type of virus is sent in an e-mail, usually as an attachment. You may not even have to open the attachment itself—some viruses will infect your computer as soon as you view the e-mail. Once opened, the virus will mail itself to all the people in your e-mail address book. Those people in turn might spread the virus to others, and so on.

SAFE SURFING

The Internet is a great tool, but it has its downsides. Protect yourself from becoming a cyber victim by following these tips.

✳ Talk with a parent about when and how you will use digital media.

✳ Never give out personal information online—such as your last name, your home address, your school, your phone number, your photos, where you hang out, or people you know—without a parent's okay.

✳ Don't share your password for your phone, e-mail, social networking sites, apps, or websites with anyone except a parent.

✳ Never agree to meet in person someone you know only online unless a parent agrees and goes with you to the meeting.

✳ Get a parent's permission before downloading an app.

✳ Always discuss which websites you visit and apps you use with a parent.

HOW does computer memory work?

Unlike a human, when a computer learns something, it remembers it forever. A computer has two types of chips that are used for computer memory. Long-term memory, called auxiliary memory, is nonvolatile—it remembers information even when the computer is shut down. Long-term memory relies on read-only memory (ROM). ROM stores the permanent information the computer needs to work, such as the operating system.

Computers also have short-term memory, called main memory. Short-term memory is volatile—it doesn't remember information once the computer is shut down. Random-access memory (RAM) is used for main memory. Main memory powers tasks or applications currently in use. It is closely connected to the computer's processor and sends and receives data quickly.

Your computer's main and auxiliary memories work together to power your machine. Here's how they do it.

1 After your computer is powered on, it runs a test to ensure everything is working properly.

2 The computer calls up the basic system that controls the screen, keyboard, and other essential components.

3 The computer moves the operating system (for instance, Windows or a Mac-based system) from ROM to RAM memory. The computer processor can now access the operating system with greater speed and efficiency.

4 When you open an application like Microsoft Word, the computer loads it to RAM. If you create a new file or open an old one, it is loaded into RAM, too. This creates a temporary storage area and allows you to work on the file.

5 Once you save the file to a storage device (hard drive or external flash drive) and close the application, it is removed from RAM.

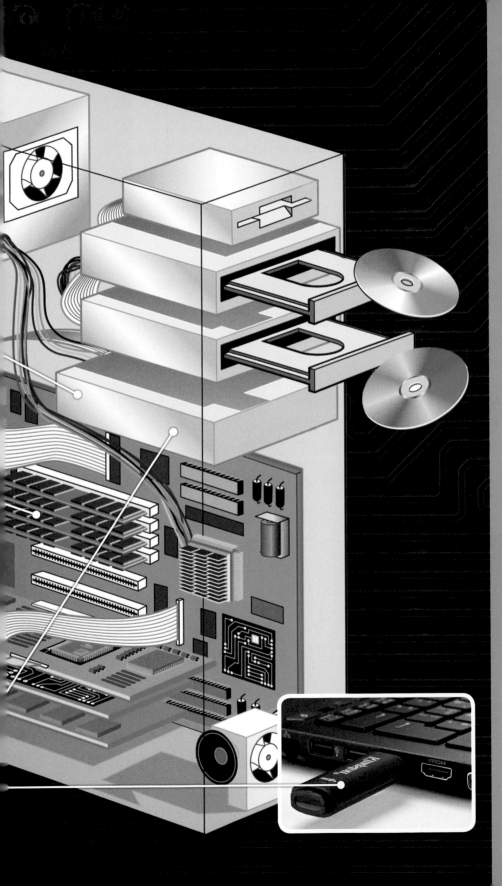

TOP TECH Early computers used magnetic tapes or disks, called hard-disk drives, to store information. Flash memory is widely used today, especially in small devices such as smartphones and laptops. Unlike hard-disk drives, flash memory has no moving parts, which makes it more durable. Like ROM, flash memory stores data even when the device is turned off. It can also erase and rewrite data quickly, like RAM.

KEEPING COUNT Computer memory is measured in bytes. A byte is the equivalent of one letter typed in a word processing program. A kilobyte is a thousand bytes, a megabyte is a million bytes, and a gigabyte is a billion bytes. For computing operations that require lots of memory, some hard drives and flash drives store data in terabytes—equal to a trillion bytes!

THEN AND NOW The ENIAC (Electronic Numerical Integrator and Computer) was the first electronic digital computer. It was two feet wide, eight feet tall, and weighed 30 tons! Despite its enormous size, it could not store any programs in its memory. This computer was only used as a calculator. Computers today can do so much more than math. They can store thousands of photos, documents, songs, and movies. Thanks to the immense power of computer memory, programs like these can fit on a thumb-sized USB.

HOW is a smartphone made?

When you're scrolling through photos or texting a friend, you're probably not thinking about how your smartphone was made. Creating a smartphone is a complex process that involves rare metals and lots of different software.

Your smartphone might be a world traveler. The Apple iPhone, for example, includes parts made in Germany, the United States, China, South Korea, Japan, and the Netherlands, among other countries. Apple has more than 200 product suppliers scattered across the globe.

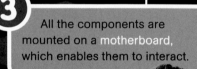

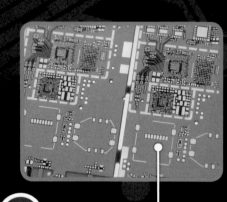

2 When the design is set, computer scientists and electrical engineers go to work assembling the hardware—the nuts and bolts of the smartphone that make it run. Hardware includes processors, batteries, camera lenses and image sensors that detect light and convert it to an electrical signal, and computer chips that allow users to do everything from surf the Internet to play music.

3 All the components are mounted on a motherboard, which enables them to interact.

1 Smartphone construction begins with design. Teams of engineers decide how the phone will look, what functions it will perform, and how all the parts will be put together. They may develop a dummy model with no functioning parts to get a sense of the phone's look and feel.

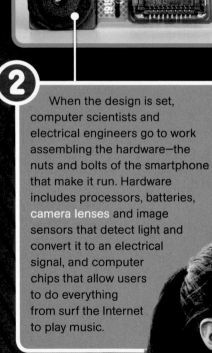

Did You Know?

Smartphones can contain more than 60 types of metals, including 16 of the 17 "rare earth elements" (REE), all of which are difficult to source. The demand for these metals can have negative environmental consequences—for instance, excessive mining that destroys landscapes. To lessen the environmental impact of your smartphone, use it as long as possible. When you do upgrade to a newer phone, donate, resell, or recycle your old phone to help recover precious metals.

CELL PHONE **DONATION BARREL**

4 Once the hardware is in place, it's ready for software. Software includes all the computer operating systems needed to run graphics, apps, and other features.

5 After the software has passed testing, the company begins to build the phones on a massive scale. Parts are sourced from many companies and assembled in factories around the world.

6 Once assembled, smartphones are tested and inspected before they are shipped to customers.

HOW TO
learn coding

Are you interested in learning the language of computers so you can make cool programs, apps, and other software for people to use? Here's a step-by-step guide for increasing your knowledge.

What to do:

1 BE CURIOUS—that's the first big step. Knowing about coding can open up a whole world of exciting possibilities, from building websites to developing apps to creating modifications, or mods, for popular games such as Minecraft. (Mods are special changes or features that coders can add to programs.)

```
13 let int: Int = 20
14 let double: Double = 3.5
15 let float: Float = 4.5
16 let bool: Bool = false
```

2 LEARN CODING LANGUAGES and their basic functions. Each language has its own syntax—specific symbols, punctuation, and key words that form its structure. Python, SQL, Java, and C are among the most popular computer languages.

3 CHECK OUT WEBSITES to read up on the basics of coding: how it works, its common applications, and handy tools to make coding easier. *Code.org* is a nonprofit organization aimed at expanding computer literacy for students worldwide. It offers online courses in computer science fundamentals, app development, game programming, and other coding-related skills. *Codecademy.com, codeconquest. com,* and *Scratch.mit.edu* (affiliated with the Massachusetts Institute of Technology) are other places to check out.

4 TRY ONE OF *CODE.ORG'S* HOUR OF CODE EVENTS. These are hour-long group tutorials on the fundamentals of coding and computer science for students of all ages. They have been organized in more than 180 countries worldwide. President Barack Obama participated in an Hour of Code event in 2014.

5 JOIN A ROBOTICS CLUB at your school or in your community. Coding is a big part of robotics, and being part of a team can give you a good incentive to improve your coding skills. NASA's Robotics Alliance Project supports national robotics competitions and provides information on robotics as well as suggested projects.

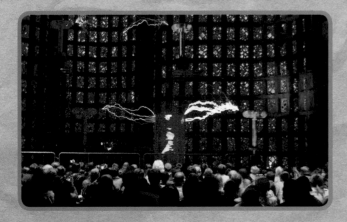

6 TAKE YOUR SKILLS TO THE NEXT LEVEL by exploring the maker world—a grassroots movement of people who like to design, create, and share their own inventions. Maker Faires are held throughout the year in locations worldwide. Computer programmers may be on hand to help people turn their computer-based ideas into reality by translating them into code. At a Maker Faire in New York City, a combination of computer technology, robotics, and Tesla coils generated a musical performance that was electric!

Here are some major terms to know for coding studies:

Language: A set of vocabulary and rules that communicates information and instructions to a computer so that it will perform specific tasks

Program: A series of instructions that tells a computer how to accomplish a certain function

Developer: A person who designs, programs, and evaluates computer software

Hardware: The physical elements of a computer, such as the circuit board, monitor, and disk drive

Software: The programs installed on a computer that control how it operates

Did You Know?

Computers can be found nearly everywhere—from schools to businesses to the family car. Scientists and engineers have been using coding and computer programming for decades. The *Apollo 11* spacecraft that went to the moon in 1969 was equipped with a computer operating system that allowed astronauts to navigate using simple commands. Considering what a complex task this was, you might be amazed to learn that your smartphone has more computing power than the *Apollo* spacecraft did.

CHAPTER 8

SPACE

HOW does the sun stay hot?

The temperature of the sun's surface is about 10,000°F. At its core, the sun is more than 27,000,000°F. The ancient Greeks believed the sun's heat came from a huge lump of coal that burned in its center. In the 1800s, some scientists thought the sun was filled with erupting volcanoes. Others believed the sun got hot from millions of meteorites striking it.

The sun started out as a massive ball of gas and dust. About 4.6 billion years ago, gravity squeezed the particles together so tightly they produced heat—and the sun was born. But how does it continue to burn? The intense heat during the birth of the sun started a process inside it called nuclear fusion.

Nuclear fusion happens when hydrogen atoms in the sun's core fuse, or combine, to form the element helium. This releases energy, which reaches Earth (93 million miles away) mostly in the form of light and heat. The sun has plenty of hydrogen, so it should keep us warm for about 5 billion more years.

6 **CORONA** The top layer of very hot gases stretches millions of miles into space.

People have always had their eyes on the skies. But thanks to powerful telescopes, space probes, and brave astronauts, our knowledge of heavenly bodies is at an all-time high.

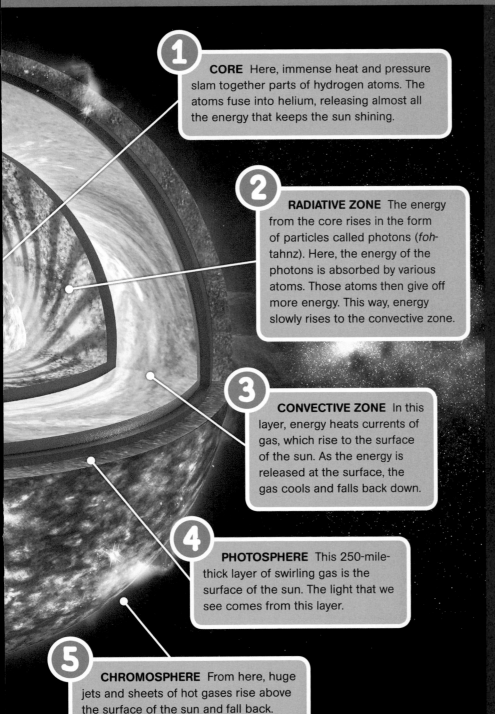

1 **CORE** Here, immense heat and pressure slam together parts of hydrogen atoms. The atoms fuse into helium, releasing almost all the energy that keeps the sun shining.

2 **RADIATIVE ZONE** The energy from the core rises in the form of particles called photons (*foh-tahnz*). Here, the energy of the photons is absorbed by various atoms. Those atoms then give off more energy. This way, energy slowly rises to the convective zone.

3 **CONVECTIVE ZONE** In this layer, energy heats currents of gas, which rise to the surface of the sun. As the energy is released at the surface, the gas cools and falls back down.

4 **PHOTOSPHERE** This 250-mile-thick layer of swirling gas is the surface of the sun. The light that we see comes from this layer.

5 **CHROMOSPHERE** From here, huge jets and sheets of hot gases rise above the surface of the sun and fall back.

SUN SAFETY

Sunlight is the reason there's life on Earth. But sunlight's ultraviolet (UV) rays can also give you a sunburn. Follow these tips to keep your skin safe during the day.

* Stay in the shade, especially between 10 a.m. and 4 p.m., when the sun's rays are strongest.

* Whenever you're out in the sun, even for a short walk, wear sunscreen with at least an SPF 30 rating. Use it year-round, not just in the summer.

* When you're outside, cover up. Wear clothes that sunlight can't go through. Place a hand inside the clothes: if you can see your hand, the cloth isn't thick enough.

* Protect your eyes. Wear sunglasses with labels that say the glasses have 100% UV protection. Wear a wide-brim hat that shades your eyes, ears, and face.

* Don't forget your lips: apply a lip balm that has an SPF of at least 15.

121

HOW do astronauts train?

Since the early days of space exploration, astronauts have landed on the moon, walked in space, performed experiments on the space shuttle, and spent time on the International Space Station (ISS).

Here's a look at some of the training astronauts get at the Lyndon B. Johnson Space Center in Houston, Texas. Some of these astronauts may one day visit the moon—or blast off for Mars.

To experience weightlessness, astronauts ride on airplanes that go high up and then dive. For 20 to 25 seconds at a time, astronauts float around the cabin in zero-gravity conditions.

Did You Know?

To become a U.S. astronaut, you must meet certain requirements.

* An astronaut must be a college graduate, with a major in engineering, math, or science.

* Many astronauts are pilots in the military, but civilians who have never flown can be astronauts, too. These astronauts are called mission specialists, and they can be engineers, scientists, doctors, or researchers.

* An astronaut must be between five feet two inches and six feet four inches tall, and be a U.S. citizen.

Crews of astronauts practice living and working in mock-ups—exact copies of the spacecraft they'll fly. They also train in simulators that reproduce the events of a mission. Trainers give astronauts problems to solve or simulate emergency situations to overcome.

Candidates receive survival training. They are taught how to stay alive if their craft lands in the ocean or in a forest. They experience tough challenges so they know what to do in a real situation.

Astronauts train for hours in huge tanks of water, which gives the feel of weightlessness. They do tasks in the water that they will do in zero gravity during spaceflight. One tank, the Neutral Buoyancy Laboratory, is more than 200 feet long and 40 feet deep. It's the largest indoor pool in the world.

SPIN CYCLE At space camp in Huntsville, Alabama, campers can train the way astronauts do. A ride on this multi-axis trainer (MAT) recreates the tumbling and spinning of a spacecraft's reentry into Earth's atmosphere.

The people on the ground who give information and instructions to astronauts during missions are called the flight control team. An astronaut crew practices an upcoming mission with a particular flight control team. That way, the actual flight will run smoothly.

HOW does the universe make stars?

The right set of ingredients and circumstances have to come together just so to create a star. Low-mass stars, like our sun, burn slowly and may last for billions or trillions of years.

3 The compression creates heat. When the heat of the protostar reaches 10,000,000° Kelvin (about 18,000,000°F), the real action begins. (Kelvin measures thermodynamics—the use or production of heat.) The incredible heat fuses (combines) the atoms of the gases. Each act of fusion creates enormous amounts of energy and light. A protostar becomes a main sequence star.

2 Once a chunk of dust and gas reaches a certain size, the gravity at its center pulls it inward and compresses it to form a protostar.

BILLIONS OF YEARS

LOW-MASS STAR LIFE CYCLE

1 In the darkness of space, a dust cloud—made mostly of old stars—floats by. Hydrogen and helium gases surround the cloud, and small chunks of dust combine with the gases. As this cloud, called a nebula, grows, its gravity increases, and it pulls in even more dust and gas.

THIS STAR IS A STAR The sun is a yellow dwarf star and the most famous low-mass star in the Milky Way. It has about 5 billion years to go before it runs out of fuel and becomes a red giant. Here are other vital sun stats.

Age: 4.6 billion years

Earth-sun distance: 93 million miles

Rotation on its axis: 25 days at its equator

Diameter: 109 times the diameter of Earth

Mass: 333,000 times the weight of Earth

6 A dwarf star is a main-sequence star of relatively small size and low brightness. A white dwarf is the hot core of the former star that remains. Remnants of stars gather in dust clouds that become nebulae, and the cycle begins again.

Fast Fact
The sun contains 99.8% of all matter in our solar system. It is so vast that 1.3 million Earths could fit inside it.

4 Like all things, a star has a life span . . . a very, very long one. After billions of years, the fuel in the star runs out. A large, older star grows into a dimmer, larger red giant.

5 As a star dies, it throws off its outer layers as a planetary nebula.

A SECOND PATH
A massive star is one that is more than eight to 10 times the mass of our sun. This type of star follows a different, shorter life cycle. It grows much bigger, forming a red supergiant. It may survive for millions of years, ending in an explosion called a supernova. Remnants may form black holes or neutron stars, or they gather in dust clouds that become nebulae once again.

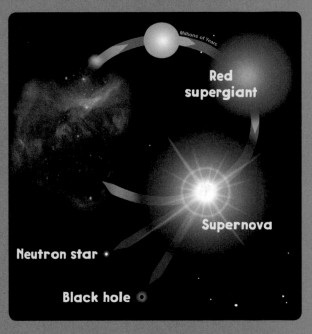

Millions of Years

Red supergiant

Supernova

Neutron star

Black hole

STAR PAIRS
Most star systems contain more than one star. The most common formation is binary, a system of two stars (*bini* means "two together"). Both stars orbit around a common center, or one orbits around the other.

HOW did the Juno probe uncover Jupiter's secrets?

Jupiter is the largest planet in the solar system, and it holds some big secrets. On July 4, 2016, scientists finally had a way to learn about some of them. The Juno space probe reached orbit around Jupiter after a five-year journey from Earth. Packed with instruments, Juno was able to send back pictures and data. One of the first discoveries scientists made was that huge storms swirl on Jupiter's poles. They saw a full infrared picture, which captured a wavelength of light that is not visible to humans. It showed the deep layers of Jupiter. And they witnessed Jupiter's moons up close. Juno is still up there, so more discoveries await.

STORMS Images of Jupiter's south pole taken by the spacecraft's camera, JunoCam, show Earth-sized polar cyclones.

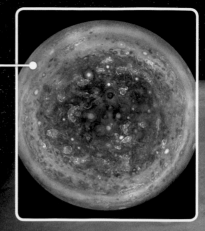

POWER The spacecraft gets its power from solar panels. They stretch out more than 66 feet to gather sunlight that's 25 times weaker than the light striking Earth.

BUILDING JUNO NASA scientists put together the Juno spacecraft. They hope it will help reveal the history of Jupiter and the solar system.

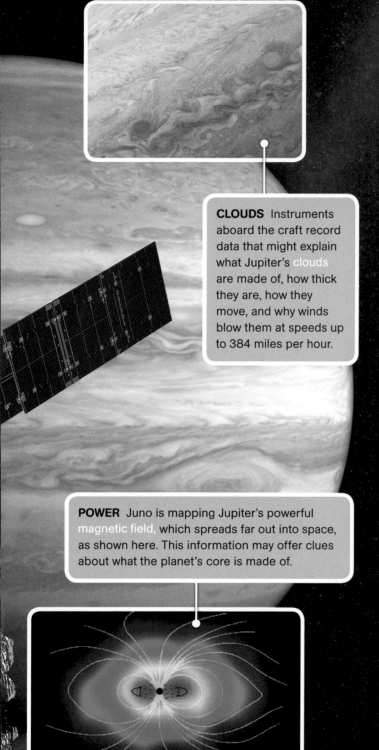

CLOUDS Instruments aboard the craft record data that might explain what Jupiter's clouds are made of, how thick they are, how they move, and why winds blow them at speeds up to 384 miles per hour.

FACT FILE: JUPITER

Jupiter is the largest planet of the solar system. Covered by swirling clouds, the planet is made mostly of hydrogen and helium in the form of gas and liquid. Here are more facts about the fifth planet from the sun.

Diameter: **88,846 miles (11 times greater than Earth's diameter)**

Average distance from the sun: **483,638,564 miles**

Average distance from Earth: **391,463,851 miles**

Average surface temperature: **−234°F**

Surface gravity: **2.4 times that of Earth**

Length of day: **9.93 hours**

Length of year: **11.87 Earth years**

Number of moons: **67**

Number of rings: **3**

Jupiter's four largest moons

POWER Juno is mapping Jupiter's powerful magnetic field, which spreads far out into space, as shown here. This information may offer clues about what the planet's core is made of.

Fast Fact

Jupiter is the oldest planet in our solar system. By taking close-up images and measurements, scientists can look back nearly to the beginning of the solar system. Jupiter's interior and its magnetic field will provide more clues to how it formed and evolved.

HOW do scientists map the galaxy?

A map is a great tool that helps you get around on Earth. It tells you where things are and shows you the different routes for getting where you need to go. But creating a map of a neighborhood and making one of the *entire Milky Way galaxy* are two very different undertakings. In recent years, scientists have made huge strides in creating maps of our home in the universe. In the process, they have found many new things to study . . . far, far away!

THE BIG PICTURE NASA's Wide-field Infrared Survey Explorer (also called the WISE spacecraft) uses infrared sensors and a telescope to take pictures from outer space. In 2015, the WISE spacecraft sent images of the Milky Way that enabled astronomers to create a more accurate map of our galaxy.

Our galaxy, called the Milky Way, is made up of four major arms—Sagittarius, Scutum-Centaurus, Perseus, and Outer—that move in a spiral from the center. Our solar system is near the Perseus arm.

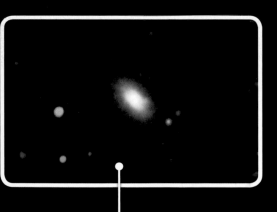

This WISE image indicates that star formations start at the center of a galaxy, which then grows from the inside out.

The WISE telescope mapped the Milky Way's central bulge of stars, which resembles a letter X.

A CLOSER LOOK

A CLOSER LOOK With a general map of the Milky Way established, it was time for a close-up. A telescope called Gaia (for Global Astrometric Interferometer for Astrophysics, although the mission now uses an optical telescope design) was launched in 2013. The goal is to create a precise 3D map of our galaxy. In operation until 2019, Gaia is tasked with studying a billion stars and other celestial objects.

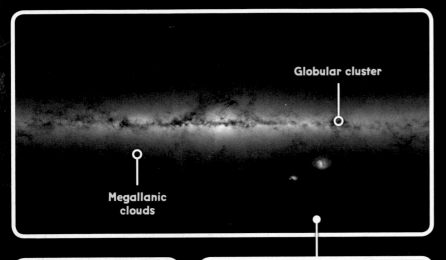

Globular cluster

Megallanic clouds

The Milky Way is brighter where there are more stars and darker where there are fewer stars. This Gaia image shows Magellanic clouds and globular clusters (dense groups of stars), too.

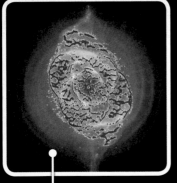

Gaia captured great detail in this image of the Cat's Eye Nebula.

Gaia spacecraft in orbit (artist's rendering)

SPACE JUNK

SPACE JUNK Much closer to Earth is another group of objects that scientists map. Many of them weren't made in space, however—they were made on Earth. More than 500,000 tiny pieces of space debris (duh-*bree*) spin around our planet. The junk comes mostly from trash and used or discarded parts of spacecraft. Most pieces of debris are tiny, smaller than a thumbnail. Some, however, are as large as grapefruits and could cause considerable damage if they collided with a spacecraft. Scientists work to keep track of all this junk to avoid such collisions.

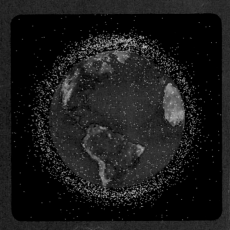

The white dots show space debris being tracked.

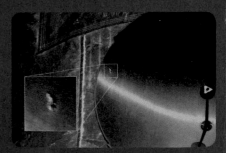

The Hubble telescope antenna dish was hit by space debris.

129

HOW does a giant telescope see hundreds of objects at once?

When you gaze up at the night sky, hundreds or even thousands of tiny points of light are visible. These lights are stars, planets, moons, and other celestial bodies. To get a handle on what's out there, scientists and astronomers need a detailed view of these objects, some of which are billions of miles away. That's where giant, powerful telescopes come in.

MEET THE KECKS Two of the largest telescopes on Earth stand atop Mauna Kea, a volcanic mountain in Hawaii. The W. M. Keck Observatory telescopes weigh 300 tons each. The primary mirrors are nearly 33 feet in diameter. Astronomers point them at the heavens, and computers direct the telescopes to follow objects and take in their light. Light is made up of different wavelengths, and each wavelength reveals something different about an object.

ADVANCED IMAGING

Like lenses on a camera, the following Keck instruments can be placed in or on the telescopes to send back different information and observations.

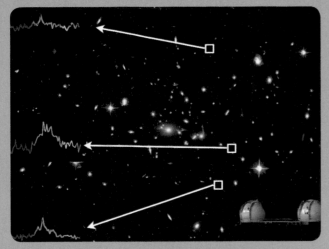

The DEIMOS (Deep Extragalactic Imaging Multi-Object Spectrograph) is a special filter that allows the telescopes to take in light from more than 1,200 galaxies in a single image. And yes, computers count all those tiny lights!

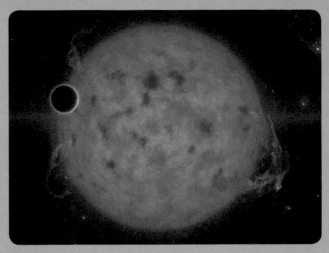

The HIRES (High Resolution Echelle Spectrometer) device measures the different colors of light from the stars and other objects. It has been key to finding exoplanets (planets outside our solar system).

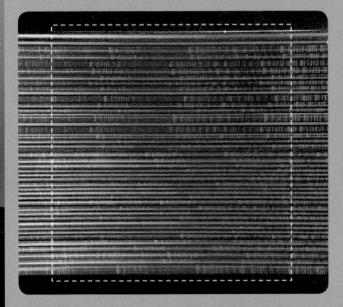

The LRIS (Low Resolution Imaging Spectrograph) filter helps Keck find objects that are farthest away from Earth. The long horizontal lines indicate objects and the shorter vertical lines show where the night sky is bright.

The NIRC (Near Infrared Camera) is perfect for gaining views of much closer objects, such as planets or the moon. The OSIRIS (OH-Suppressing Infrared Imaging Spectrograph) takes pictures of tiny slices of the sky. This helps scientists track very distant, and thus very faint, objects. OH stands for molecules of oxygen and hydrogen that are in the atmosphere. This instrument helps keep those gases from disturbing the telescopes' view.

HOW TO
launch a rocket

Remember to ask an adult for help.

The first rockets ever launched were fireworks, set off in China more than a thousand years ago. The fireworks used the power of gunpowder to take off. It wasn't until the mid-1900s that people began to build rockets to travel into space. A space rocket needs a lot of power to lift off and escape Earth's gravity. The power comes from huge engines that burn tons of liquid fuel—often a combination of liquid oxygen and liquid hydrogen. As the gases push out the bottom of the rocket, the ship rises. But you can launch a rocket with something as simple as air power.

What you need:

- Plastic tennis ball can with lid, or plastic soda bottle with cap
- Three different types of soda straws: flexible, jumbo, and superjumbo (Superjumbo straws can be found in places that sell milk shakes, such as diners and fast food restaurants.)
- Large pencil
- Scissors
- Tape
- Paper

Fast Fact
In 1926, American scientist Robert Goddard launched the first liquid-fueled rocket. Thanks to his work and that of others, rockets now send astronauts, satellites, and probes into space.

What to do:

1 Poke a hole in the lid of the plastic can, or the cap of the plastic bottle, with the large pencil or the pair of scissors. Have an adult help you.

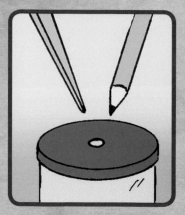

2 Cut the end of the flexible straw on an angle. Push it through the hole in the lid. The straw should fit snugly. Put the lid back on the can.

3 Stick the jumbo straw over the end of the flex straw. Tape it in place.

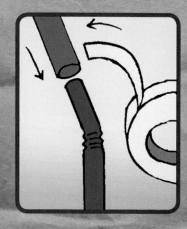

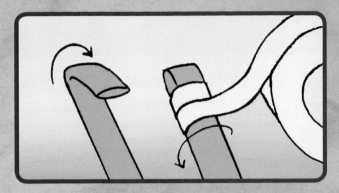

④ Make a rocket by folding over half an inch of the end of the superjumbo straw. Tape down the end.

⑥ Slide the superjumbo straw over the jumbo launcher straw. Aim, then give the can a sharp squeeze. Watch your rocket blast off.

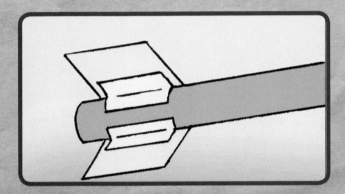

⑤ Make fins from paper to help your rocket fly straight. Tape two or three fins to the superjumbo straw.

HOW IT WORKS

Air pressure, not burning gases, makes your rocket take off. When you squeeze the can or bottle, the air inside the straw is compressed into a smaller space. This causes the pressure in the container to increase. To release the pressure, air rushes out the open end of the jumbo straw, causing the superjumbo straw to fly up and away—just like a real rocket.

Assembling *Orion*

NEXT STOP, MARS! NASA is building the new *Orion* rocket, complete with a crew capsule, to help carry the first astronauts to Mars. Testing is underway now to send the unpiloted *Orion* to an asteroid in the 2020s. If all goes well, a trip to Mars is scheduled for the 2030s. Could one of those astronauts be you?

Testing spacesuits

CHAPTER 9

THE HUMAN BODY

HOW does the body fight germs?

Germs are all around you. Most are harmless, but a few can make you sick. When bacteria, viruses, and other microorganisms (tiny one-celled life-forms) try to infect you, your immune system springs into action. To be immune is to be protected, and the immune system has several ways to fight germs and keep you healthy. The first line of defense is your skin, which keeps out germs. The natural openings in the body, such as the mouth and eyes, produce chemicals to kill germs. If germs do get through your outer defenses, they are attacked by different types of white blood cells.

When you are infected, you feel sick: glands in the neck or armpits get swollen and tender, your temperature rises, skin that is cut might get red and sore. These are signs that your body is battling the germs.

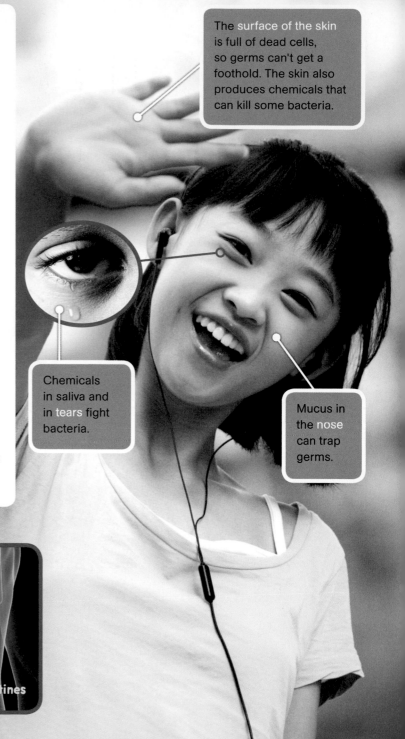

The surface of the skin is full of dead cells, so germs can't get a foothold. The skin also produces chemicals that can kill some bacteria.

Chemicals in saliva and in tears fight bacteria.

Mucus in the nose can trap germs.

Stomach acid kills bacteria.

Stomach

Intestines

The human body is an amazing, complicated machine. It doesn't come with an instruction manual, but we know a lot about how the parts work and how to keep them running.

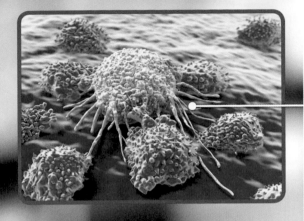

White blood cells, or lymphocytes, patrol the body, looking for germs to kill. There are three main types: Natural Killer (NK) cells, T cells, and B cells. NK cells can tell the difference between normal cells and cells infected by viruses or tumors. When they recognize invaders, they release granules that attack and kill the invading cells.

Human T and B cells identify pathogens and toxins. They produce memory cells that remember pathogens the body encounters, preparing the body for a strong response if any of those pathogens appear again. Memory cells are packed with mitochondria, which helps them live a long time.

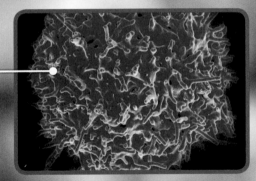

Phagocytes are also white blood cells. They are prompted by lymphocytes to swallow and destroy invading cells.

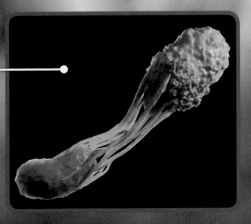

KEEP HEALTHY

The immune system works hard to fight off germs and keep you healthy. But there are ways you can pitch in and help out your body's defenses.

Get enough sleep. You should be getting nine to 10 hours of sleep every night.

Eat right. Try to eat three regular meals of nutritious foods that include fruits, vegetables, and whole grains. Avoid sugary foods and drinks, as well as fast food. Drink plenty of water.

Exercise. When you exercise, you strengthen your bones, muscles, and heart, and make the lungs work better.

Wash your hands regularly. Regular handwashing is the best way to stop germs from spreading. Wash with warm water and soap for 20 seconds—the time it takes to sing "Happy Birthday."

Reduce stress. Too much stress over a long period of time can weaken the immune system. Talk over your problems with your parents or teachers. To reduce stress, you can exercise, enjoy hobbies, read for pleasure, or play with a pet.

HOW do wounds heal?

You and your friends are having a blast, but then—whammo!—you fall and cut your knee. Almost immediately, your body leaps into action. A series of fortunate events takes place to stop the cut from bleeding and allow the healing to begin.

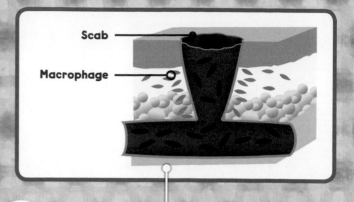

Scab

Macrophage

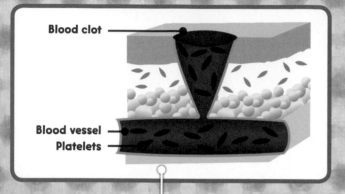

Blood clot

Blood vessel
Platelets

3 **REPAIR WORK!** Once the clot has formed, blood vessels open wide so nutrients and oxygen can reach the site of the injury quickly. This widening causes inflammation, or swelling, around the wound. At the same time, white blood cells called macrophages work to fight off infection, stimulate cell growth, and repair the wound.

1 **CALL TO ACTION!** First, the blood vessels around the wound tighten to slow the bleeding. Next, damaged cells within the blood vessels release chemicals that bring platelets to the scene of the injury. Platelets are disk-shaped cells present throughout the blood. The platelets stick together in layers to form a blood clot, or plug, for the wound.

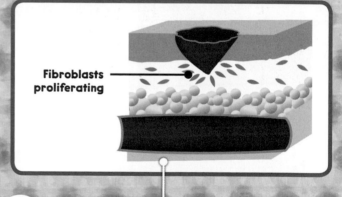

Fibroblasts
proliferating

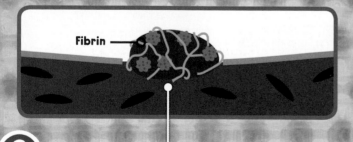

Fibrin

2 The clot helps keep bacteria out and stop blood loss. A protein called fibrin is activated. Fibrin is stringy and flexible. It forms a blood-stopping mesh over the cut.

4 **TIME TO REBUILD!** Fibroblast cells produce a fiberlike protein called collagen. Collagen acts like scaffolding, or a temporary framework, during cell growth. The collagen fibers are cross-linked over one another until they form a stable scar. During this phase, cells on the outer layer of skin also divide to form new skin. Over time, the collagen rearranges itself to look as it did before, but if the wound was big enough, a scar will remain.

HOW TO HELP A WOUND HEAL

If you or a friend is injured, always have an adult administer first aid. If you fall on the playground, see the school nurse. If you topple off your bike in the driveway and scrape your knees, let your parents know. And if a wound is severe, get medical attention right away.

Here are some first aid tips for treating cuts and scrapes.

✳ Wash hands before touching the injured area, to help prevent infection.

✳ If bleeding does not stop on its own, apply gentle pressure with a clean cloth and elevate the wound.

✳ Rinse the wound with water. Clean the area around it with soap and a fresh washcloth. If debris—a splinter, for example—is in the wound, show an adult. He or she may sterilize tweezers with alcohol and gently remove the debris, or you may need to see a doctor.

✳ Apply antibiotic ointment.

✳ Cover the wound with a sterile adhesive bandage.

Did You Know?

A deep or jagged wound that exposes the muscle tissue will require stitches to close properly. In the past, these injuries were sewn closed with medical thread. Today, doctors can also use staples or a special type of surgical glue known as liquid stitches.

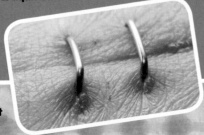

Surgical staples at work

DEEP TROUBLE   Sometimes a deep or dirty wound calls for a tetanus shot. Tetanus is a rare but serious disease caused when certain bacteria, *Clostridium tetani*, enter a wound. These bacteria are commonly found in soil, manure, and dust. If you work around animals and are injured, your doctor may recommend a tetanus shot in addition to treating the wound itself. The best way to avoid tetanus is to get regular vaccinations.

Tetanus bacteria

Watch out for rusty nails and splinters.

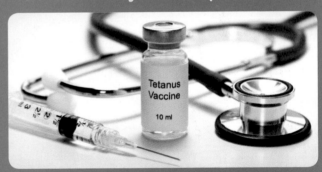

Tetanus shot Kids and adults get vaccines to protect against tetanus.

Hand washing Help protect against tetanus and other diseases by keeping your hands clean.

HOW do medicines work?

When you're feeling sick, you might need to see a doctor. After you tell the doctor what's wrong, the doctor will examine you. He or she will look into your eyes, nose, and throat, listen to your heartbeat and lungs, and take your blood pressure. Armed with information, the doctor will offer a diagnosis—the reason why you are sick—and give a treatment. Often that treatment is some kind of medicine.

A medicine is a specific chemical that treats your illness. It can be a liquid, tablet, or capsule you swallow. Liquids can also be injected with a needle right into the bloodstream. Creams or ointments are absorbed through the skin. Fluids can be dropped into the eyes or ears. Inhalers spray drugs into the nose or throat. Drugs can fight an illness, prevent an illness, or make the symptoms of an illness less strong.

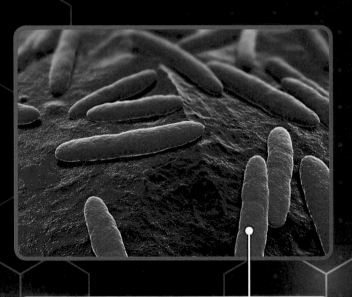

DISEASE FIGHTERS An antibiotic kills bacteria or keeps them from multiplying. Bacteria (shown here greatly magnified) are germs that can sometimes cause disease. Certain drugs also kill other types of microorganisms that can lead to disease, such as fungi and parasites. Medicine can also target cells that aren't working normally, such as cancer cells.

BE PREPARED A vaccine is made of a dead or weakened part of a germ, such as a flu virus. When a vaccine is injected into a person, the body reacts by building up defenses against that particular germ. If that type of germ one day tries to infect the person, the body will be ready to attack it right away.

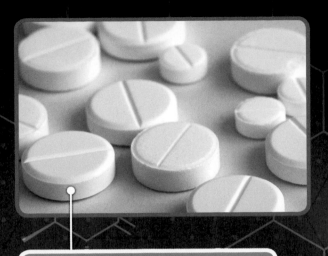

THE MOLD THAT CHANGED HISTORY

When Dr. Alexander Fleming returned from vacation in September of 1928, he found a messy laboratory—and a revolution in medicine. A mold called *Penicillium notatum* had started growing in his petri dishes. It was preventing bacteria called staphylococci from growing.

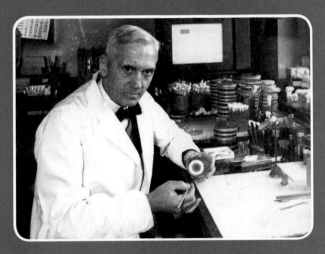

PAINKILLERS Painkillers like aspirin can make you feel better while your body heals. If a part of the body is injured, nerve endings send pain signals to the brain. The drugs interfere with the message, so the pain stops.

Dr. Fleming wrote: "When I woke up just after dawn on September 28, 1928, I certainly didn't plan to revolutionize all medicine by discovering the world's first antibiotic, or bacteria killer. But I guess that was exactly what I did."

The story didn't end there. Ten years later, Dr. Howard Florey, who was also studying uses for bacteria and mold, learned of Fleming's work. He began experimenting with fluid extracted from the mold. The penicillin, as it was called, cured infections in mice. He tried it on a human patient in 1940, who began to recover. Unfortunately, he didn't have enough penicillin to save the patient.

REPLACEMENTS Sometimes the body doesn't produce enough, or any, of a substance. Drugs can be used to replace those substances. For example, a person with a disease called diabetes gets extra insulin to stay healthy from an insulin shot. The shot comes in an insulin kit like the one in the photo.

After considerable research, in 1941, scientists determined how to produce penicillin in large quantities. During World War I, 18% of wounded soldiers died of infection. In World War II, that number dropped to just 1%. Penicillin had changed history.

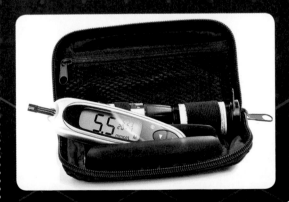

HOW does the stomach digest food?

If you gulp down too much pizza too quickly, your stomach will expand. Nerve endings in your belly tell your brain, "You're full. Stop eating!" And you do—after having that one last slice. But what is happening to the pizza you've eaten?

The slices are taking a long journey through the digestive system. After you swallow, the food goes down a tube called the esophagus (es-*ahf*-a-gus). The pizza then makes a pit stop in the stomach. The stomach is a muscular bag that crushes the food and churns it in a strong acid until the pizza turns into a souplike liquid called chyme (*kime*). The chyme sits in the stomach for two to six hours, until it's ready to move on to the intestines and out the other end.

Check out how food gets broken down in the stomach (and learn why the stomach doesn't digest itself).

MUCOUS CELLS These cells produce mucus, a thick liquid that coats the stomach lining and keeps the hydrochloric acid from touching it. The cells also produce bicarbonate. When this chemical mixes with the mucus, it turns the acid into water. Even if the stomach does get damaged by the acid, every cell in the lining is replaced every week.

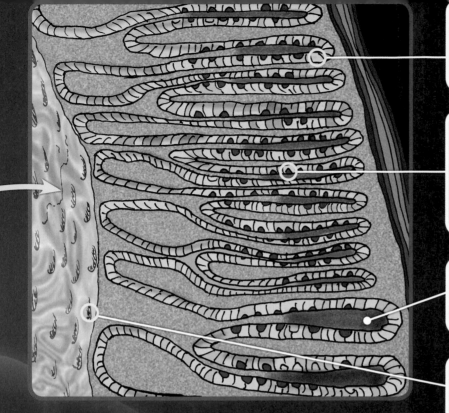

PEPSIN CELLS They produce a chemical called pepsin, which breaks down proteins and carbohydrates in food.

ACID CELLS These cells make hydrochloric acid, which turns food into liquid. Hydrochloric acid is strong enough to dissolve wood and even some metals. Too much of this can irritate the stomach lining.

GASTRIC GLANDS Hydrochloric acid and pepsin mix in narrow tubes called gastric glands.

GASTRIC PITS The mix of hydrochloric acid and pepsin flows out of the gastric glands and into the stomach through millions of tiny holes called gastric pits.

THE ECOSYSTEM INSIDE YOU Our digestive system is packed with 100 trillion microbes, most of them friendly bacteria living in the small and large intestines. They feed off the food we eat and crowd our intestines, preventing bad invader microbes from moving in.

Gut bacteria produce enzymes that help the body break down substances that our bodies alone could not digest, such as fiber and some starches and sugars. Most of the nutritional value of vegetables and fruits would be wasted without these bacteria. Certain bacteria also produce vitamin B12 and vitamin K, which are absorbed by the body.

Muscles in the digestive system move food down in a wave of automatic contractions. What was once a meal becomes a mass of undigested food called feces (*fees*-ease), along with a lot of living and dead bacteria. About half the feces is made of bacteria, which give feces its brown color.

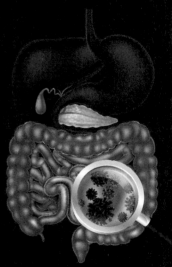

HOW does exercise build strong muscles?

The human body contains more than 600 muscles. Together, they make up about one-third of your body weight. Muscles have different tasks. Cardiac muscle pumps the heart. Smooth muscle supports blood vessels and organs such as the stomach, intestines, and bladder. Skeletal muscle holds you up and gets you moving.

To lift the arm, some muscles will contract, or shorten, and others will relax, or lengthen. Skeletal muscles come in pairs. As you curl your arm, for instance, the biceps muscle on the top of your upper arm contracts, while the triceps muscle on the underside relaxes. When you straighten your arm, the biceps muscle relaxes and the triceps muscle contracts.

MUSCLE ANATOMY

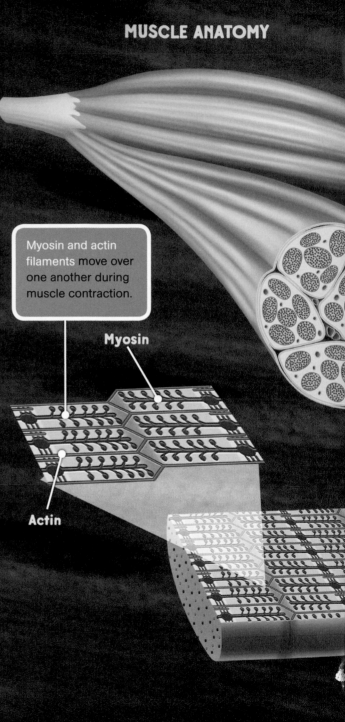

Myosin and actin filaments move over one another during muscle contraction.

Myosin

Actin

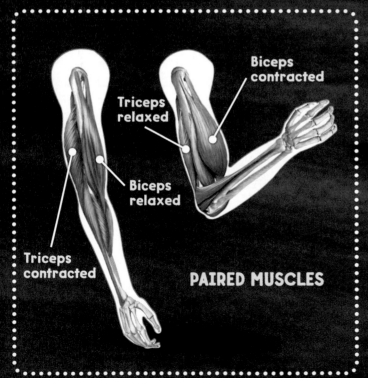

Biceps contracted

Triceps relaxed

Biceps relaxed

Triceps contracted

PAIRED MUSCLES

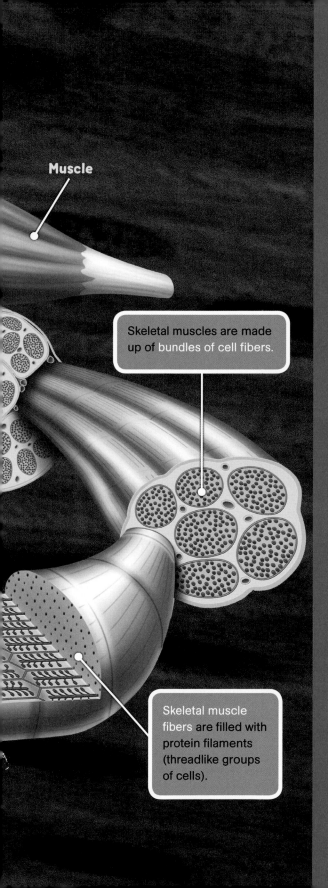

Muscle

Skeletal muscles are made up of bundles of cell fibers.

Skeletal muscle fibers are filled with protein filaments (threadlike groups of cells).

GOOD STRESS Exercises that use resistance bands, as well as sit-ups, chin-ups, and push-ups, are good ways to build muscle strength. When your muscles strain during exercise, the stress on them causes microscopic tears in the muscle. As your body repairs the damage, the result is muscle growth. Not all muscle stress is good, so always consult with a parent or doctor before starting an exercise program.

BE ACTIVE AND PLAY OUTDOORS Climbing uses different muscle groups and builds strength. Activities like running, biking, and dancing help you grow stronger, too. Exercise has another benefit. Stress to the bone plates at the end of bones stimulates growth. Why play outdoors? It's fun! And vitamin D (which your body manufactures using sunlight) helps build strong bones, which are important to physical fitness. Wear sunscreen to avoid skin damage.

HOW do eyeglasses help you see better?

The eye is an amazing and complicated organ that starts working when light passes through the cornea. The cornea is a clear shield over the eye that focuses light. After the light enters a small opening called the pupil, the lens focuses it again, but this time onto the retina at the back of the eye, where an image appears upside down. The retina is covered by cells that are sensitive to light. When the light hits the retina, the cells send electric signals to the brain. The brain unscrambles the signals to make the right-side-up image that we see.

You may take vision for granted, but eyes don't always work perfectly. Some people have trouble seeing near or far objects clearly. If things are blurry, they may need glasses or contact lenses. When they put them on or in, the world comes back into focus.

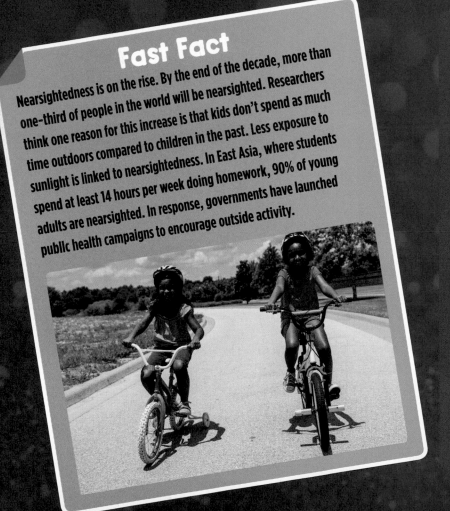

Fast Fact

Nearsightedness is on the rise. By the end of the decade, more than one-third of people in the world will be nearsighted. Researchers think one reason for this increase is that kids don't spend as much time outdoors compared to children in the past. Less exposure to sunlight is linked to nearsightedness. In East Asia, where students spend at least 14 hours per week doing homework, 90% of young adults are nearsighted. In response, governments have launched public health campaigns to encourage outside activity.

THE EYES HAVE IT To make sure your eyes stay healthy, follow these tips.

• Eat five servings of fruits and vegetables every day. Nutrients in foods such as oranges, broccoli, corn, carrots, and green, leafy vegetables will help keep your peepers perfect.

• Get plenty of exercise. Physical activity gets the blood moving, delivering more oxygen and nutrients to your eyes. But be sure to protect your eyes with goggles if you play contact sports.

• When on the computer, look away for 20 seconds every 20 minutes to avoid eyestrain. Don't sit too close to the screen. Your eyes should be about two feet away.

• Get an eye exam by a doctor at least once every two years.

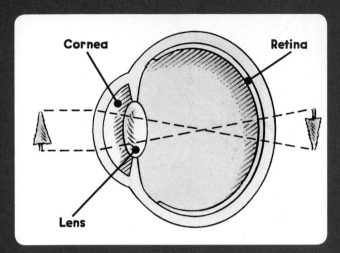

FOCUS ON THE EYES Eyeglasses and contact lenses can help correct different vision problems that affect how we see things.

FARSIGHTED A farsighted person can see objects at a distance clearly. Things that are close look fuzzy because either the eyeball is too short or the cornea is too flat. Light from near objects is focused behind the retina, not on it. Glasses or contact lenses that correct this are convex, which means they curve out slightly. This spreads the light apart and focuses it on the retina.

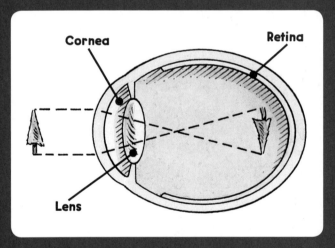

NEARSIGHTED A nearsighted person sees close objects clearly. Objects that are far away are blurry because the eyeball is too long or the cornea curves too much. The light from distant objects is focused in front of the retina. Glasses or contact lenses that correct this are concave, meaning they curve in slightly. This bends the light inward and focuses it on the retina.

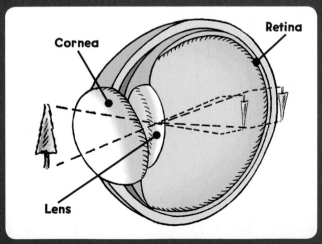

ASTIGMATISM A person with astigmatism (ah-*stig*-ma-tiz-im) may see objects both near and far out of focus. Most people's corneas are shaped like baseballs. A person with astigmatism has a cornea that looks more like a football. Light scatters, focusing on different areas of the retina. This makes objects seem wavy. To correct this problem, glasses or contact lenses focus light on the same area of the retina.

HOW do braces straighten teeth?

Crooked teeth are an inherited trait, just like hair and eye color. Thumb sucking or the overuse of bottles and pacifiers can also cause teeth to grow in the wrong direction. Fortunately, braces can straighten out a crooked smile.

Straightening teeth isn't just about looks. Crooked teeth can cause problems with eating or talking. They may lead to gum disease, because gaps between teeth give bacteria room to grow, while crowded teeth leave too little room to brush properly. When top and bottom teeth rub together, they can wear down quickly.

Did You Know?

It varies from person to person, but on average braces take one to three years to straighten teeth.

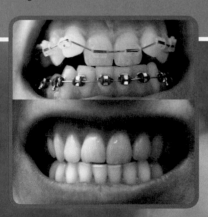

Fast Fact

Tooth enamel is like tooth armor. It is the hardest biological material there is—harder than bone, and harder even than steel. But it's brittle, which is why teeth can chip.

THE FORCE IS WITH . . . BRACES

Chewing puts (literally) tons of pressure on teeth. Stretchy, connective bands called ligaments protect teeth from chewing forces by acting as shock absorbers. When you bite down on something hard, special receptor cells in the ligaments tell the brain to stop chewing so your teeth aren't damaged.

Braces apply a steady force to teeth, slowly pulling them apart or pushing them together until they're evenly spaced. When the receptor cells (called mechanoreceptors) feel this pressure, they activate bone cells (called osteoclasts), which release acids and proteins to dissolve parts of the jawbone.

Next, the mechanoreceptors activate different bone cells, known as osteoblasts. These cells deposit minerals to form new bone and rebuild the jaw.

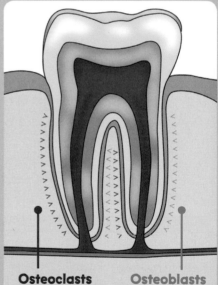

Osteoclasts dissolve bone

Osteoblasts rebuild bone

GETTING BRACES If your teeth are crooked and need to be straightened, the dentist will recommend you see a special dentist called an orthodontist.

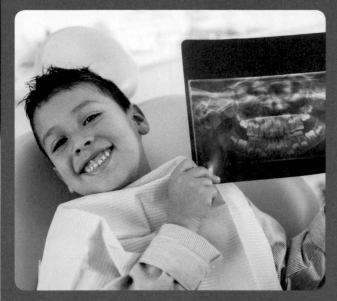

FIRST The orthodontist takes photos, molds, and X-rays of the teeth to decide the best way to fit the braces.

SECOND The orthodontist cleans and dries the teeth. He or she assembles the materials, which include brackets, arch wires, and bands.

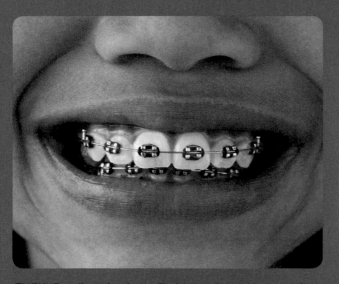

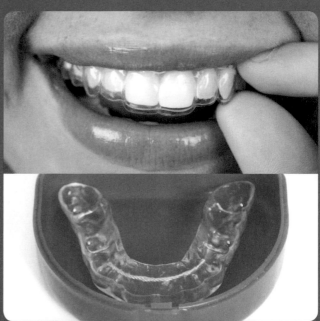

THEN Bonding glue is applied to teeth to secure teeth brackets. Arch wire, which guides the teeth, is added. Tiny rubber bands on each bracket hold the wire in place. During regular visits, the orthodontist will check the progress and may adjust the wires and bands.

FINALLY After braces come off, a removable retainer is made to fit over the teeth. The retainer holds the straightened teeth in place and prevents them from slipping back into their old positions. Sometimes a retainer is used on its own to realign teeth.

HOW TO grow salad on a windowsill

Remember to ask an adult for help.

Greens are good, and good for you. They form an important part of a balanced diet. And leafy greens grow well indoors, even in winter: try butterhead, romaine, baby oakleaf, or other lettuce varieties, or plant spinach or herbs.

You don't need lots of land to grow your own salad greens. All you need is a sunny window, a pot, a growing medium such as potting soil, and seeds. You'll be harvesting your own salads in no time!

What you need:

- Long, slim container that fits on a windowsill (the container should have holes for drainage and a tray to catch water runoff)
- Nutrient-rich potting soil, compost, or seed-starting mix
- Salad seeds
- Small trowel (a sturdy spoon will work, too)
- Watering can and mister

What to do:

1 Place your container on a windowsill. South-facing windows usually get the best light.

2 Fill the pot with soil to half an inch from the top. Don't tamp or press it down.

3 Create ruts a quarter of an inch deep and two inches apart. Sprinkle seeds along the ruts. Cover loosely with soil.

4 Water regularly, so the soil stays moist. To test whether it's time to water your seeds, stick a finger into the soil. If the soil feels dry, add water.

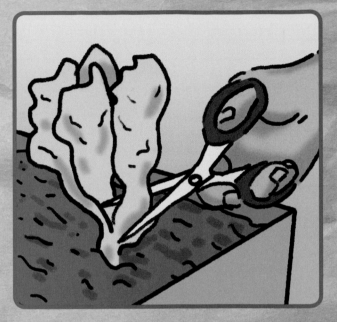

5 After the plants have sprouted, spray the soil with a mister to keep it moist, but not soaking. Seedlings should be one inch apart. If they're too crowded, remove some of the plants.

6 Once your lettuce reaches two to four inches in height, cut the outer leaves approximately one inch above the soil. New leaves will grow and be ready to harvest about two weeks later.

GOOD AND GOOD FOR YOU You can expand your windowsill garden and grow a mix of tasty, healthy foods. Here are some other things you can grow.

Tomatoes, green leafy vegetables, and peppers are packed with vitamin C, which boosts the immune system and helps wounds heal.

Carrots contain vitamin A, which protects the skin and digestive tract and prevents infection.

Radishes are good sources of fiber, which aids digestion, produces good bacteria in the gut, and helps remove toxins during elimination.

HOW do you know when information is accurate?

The Internet is made up of more than 1 billion websites. It's easy to find answers to your questions online—but are they the right answers? Anyone can publish information on the Web, from academic experts and respected journalists to biased writers to pranksters looking to trick people. (*Biased* means favoring particular ideas or people over others.) Printed information, too, is not always correct. Whom do you trust? Ask yourself important questions before deciding whether information is truthful or not.

WHO WROTE IT? Words matter, and a credible author stands by his or her writing. Look for the author's name and qualifications, which could include education, professional training, and other articles or books published under the author's name.

WHO PUBLISHED IT? Anyone can purchase Internet domain names that end in *.com*, *.org*, or *.net*. Nonprofit organizations that use *.org* may be trying to influence your opinions, although that doesn't necessarily mean their information isn't factual. Universities use *.edu*, and government agencies use *.gov*—these are generally trustworthy sources. So are reputable news organizations and book publishers.

IS IT STILL TRUE? Look for a publication date and updates to data. Make sure information is current.

WHERE DID THE INFORMATION COME FROM? A credible article often includes sources, or references to books, articles, or research. Primary sources are firsthand accounts— such as historical diaries, original documents, and photographs.

WHY WAS IT WRITTEN? The author's intent could be to sway readers into feeling a certain way about a subject or event. Be wary of emotional language and writing that tells only part of a story.

PHOTO FRAUD Colors can be altered, and images can be changed or combined to create something different from the originals. Sometimes the goal is to fool people, but sometimes images are enhanced to convey information. Can you pick the fake?

If you said the elephant, you're right—someone used a computer to combine a photo background, a painting of an elephant, and a jump rope. But the asteroid, below, has been altered, too. A telescope took the photo in black-and-white, and scientists added colors to explain to viewers what they are seeing—blue shows "young terrain" on a very old rock. A reputable source, like NASA, will make it clear that the colors are added, not real.

ORLD

The world is a great big, wonderful place, and you're part of it. Learn how schools can use the sun's energy, see what it takes to campaign for a cause, discover why every species matters, and more.

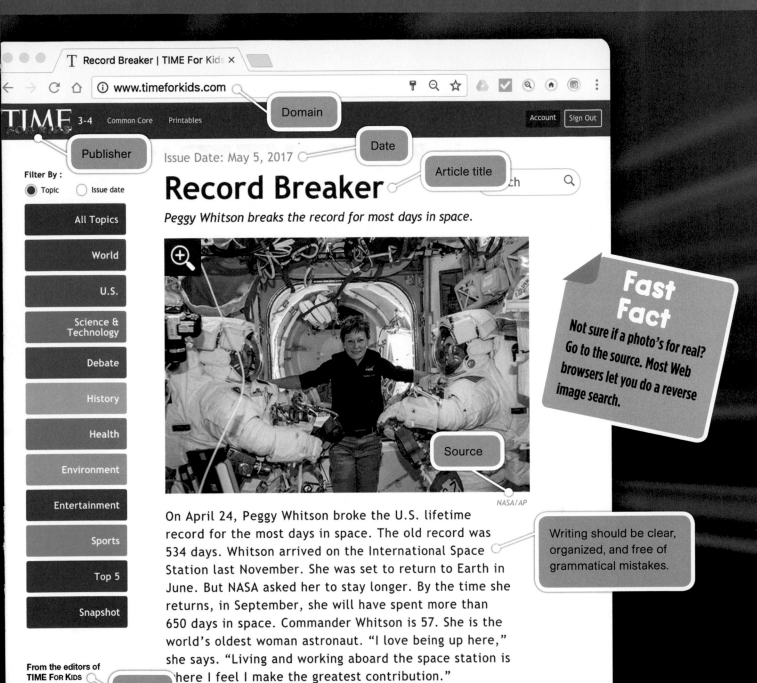

T Record Breaker | TIME For Kids ×

www.timeforkids.com

Domain

TIME 3-4   Common Core   Printables   Account   Sign Out

Publisher

Date

Issue Date: May 5, 2017

Article title

Filter By :
○ Topic   ○ Issue date

Record Breaker

Peggy Whitson breaks the record for most days in space.

All Topics

World

U.S.

Science & Technology

Debate

History

Health

Environment

Entertainment

Sports

Top 5

Snapshot

Source

NASA / AP

Fast Fact
Not sure if a photo's for real? Go to the source. Most Web browsers let you do a reverse image search.

On April 24, Peggy Whitson broke the U.S. lifetime record for the most days in space. The old record was 534 days. Whitson arrived on the International Space Station last November. She was set to return to Earth in June. But NASA asked her to stay longer. By the time she returns, in September, she will have spent more than 650 days in space. Commander Whitson is 57. She is the world's oldest woman astronaut. "I love being up here," she says. "Living and working aboard the space station is where I feel I make the greatest contribution."

Writing should be clear, organized, and free of grammatical mistakes.

From the editors of **TIME FOR KIDS**

Author

Contact Us   FAQ   Privacy Policy   Your California Privacy Rights   Terms of Service

HOW does saving one species help our planet?

When the first group of gray wolves was relocated to Yellowstone National Park in 1995, biologists knew that these top predators would play a key role in the ecosystem. Yet even the scientists didn't anticipate how big the impact would be when the wolves—absent from the park for 70 years—were turned loose.

What happened was an ecological chain of events that started at the top of the food chain and trickled all the way down. (Scientists call this a trophic cascade.) Researchers have witnessed such events only a few times in history. Clearly, saving just one species can make a difference to the well-being of a local environment, and to our planet in general.

Did You Know?

In the 1800s, as the United States expanded westward, settlers saw wolves as a threat to livestock. Landowners and farmers, with encouragement from the government, killed wolves with poisoned meat. By the 1930s, no wolves lived in Yellowstone. By the 1960s, just 300 wolves remained in the continental United States.

AT FIRST

During 1995 and 1996, 31 gray wolves were relocated to Yellowstone from Canada. Over the next two decades, that population grew to about 100. Wolves hunt elk for food. When there were no wolves in Yellowstone, elk populations had exploded. Elk graze along rivers and in meadows, where they eat and also trample young willow, aspen, and cottonwood saplings. This loss of vegetation had taken a toll on beavers, which need the trees to survive, especially in winter. Spooked by the wolves' presence, elk broke into smaller groups and scattered throughout the park.

Fast Fact

In 1973, Congress passed the Endangered Species Act, which protects wolves, among many other species of plants and animals. It took more than 20 years for conservationists to complete the task of restoring wolves to Yellowstone.

CHANGING WATERWAYS

As the elk herds dispersed, saplings were able to grow into stands of trees that provided beavers with their food source. Beavers built new dams in ponds, rivers, and streams. Songbirds, such as this Wilson's warbler, nested in willow trees. Otters, muskrats, ducks, and fish were drawn to the cold, shaded water.

COMPETITION IS GOOD

Wolves also hunt coyotes. With fewer coyotes around, the hawks, weasels, foxes, and badgers are able to compete and catch numbers of rabbits and mice.

LIFE IN BALANCE

Many animals make meals out of the wolves' leftovers (called carrion). Scavenger birds and bears feed on carrion left by wolves. While the wolves do take life, an ecosystem in balance also gives life.

HOW do plants get energy?

All living things need food to survive. Unlike animals, most plants can make their own food, through a process called photosynthesis. Organisms that create their own food are called autotrophs (*auto* means "self" and *trophe* means "feeding"). The three main ingredients of photosynthesis are sunlight, water, and carbon dioxide. Here's how photosynthesis works.

Plants take in carbon dioxide from the air.

3 Carbon dioxide enters the plant through stomata, or holes, usually on the undersides of leaves. The hydrogen and oxygen atoms of water combine with the carbon from carbon dioxide to form a carbohydrate, also known as sugar. The sugar is sent to the rest of the plant as food.

The plant draws up water and minerals from the ground through its roots.

Stomata

Fast Fact

The way plants make sugar using the sun's energy can be written out as a scientific equation: H_2O (water) + CO_2 (carbon dioxide) = $C_6H_{12}O_6$ (sugars) + O_2 (oxygen). H stands for hydrogen, O for oxygen, and C for carbon.

Minerals

Sunlight

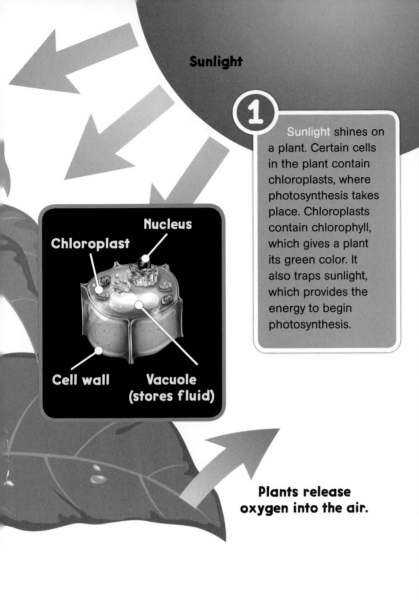

①

Sunlight shines on a plant. Certain cells in the plant contain chloroplasts, where photosynthesis takes place. Chloroplasts contain chlorophyll, which gives a plant its green color. It also traps sunlight, which provides the energy to begin photosynthesis.

Chloroplast

Nucleus

Cell wall

Vacuole (stores fluid)

Plants release oxygen into the air.

②

A plant absorbs water through its roots. Each water molecule contains two hydrogen atoms and one oxygen atom.

Water

How is food transported throughout a plant?

A plant cell that produces sugar is called a sugar source. A plant uses a special tissue called phloem to transport the sugar, along with minerals, to areas known as sugar sinks. A sink can be an area of the plant that is growing; an organ that cannot create its own food, such as a root; or a leaf or fruit. Whenever a plant needs sugar—for instance, at night when photosynthesis doesn't happen—the sugar sink becomes a sugar source.

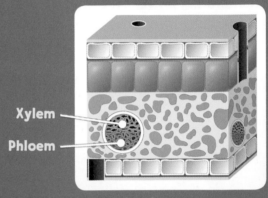

Xylem

Phloem

Leaf anatomy

As sugar moves into the phloem, water naturally follows, by a process called osmosis. Osmosis allows the sugar-filled water to flow into and out of cells. The sugary water solution that results is commonly called sap. Unlike the xylem, which can only carry water upward, phloem carries sap upward and downward. The water flow causes pressure, moving sap to wherever it's needed. As long as a plant has sunlight, water, carbon dioxide, and nutritious minerals, it can fend for itself.

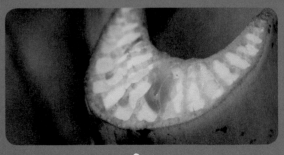

Sap

HOW do wind turbines make electricity?

Wind can sometimes be a destructive force. But wind is also a great help to humans. Over the centuries, windmills have been used to pump water, drain lakes, cut wood, and grind grain. Today, a kind of windmill, called a wind turbine, is being used to produce electricity. Wind is a renewable energy—it will never run out. Wind turbines don't cause pollution and are cheap to run. Countries around the world are increasingly using wind to fulfill energy needs.

In May 2017, the world's largest wind turbines—with 260-foot-long blades—began generating power off the coast of Liverpool, England. As turbines increase in size, the cost of generating electricity decreases. Today's turbines have an 8 megawatt (MW) capacity, but 12 MW models will be built in the near future.

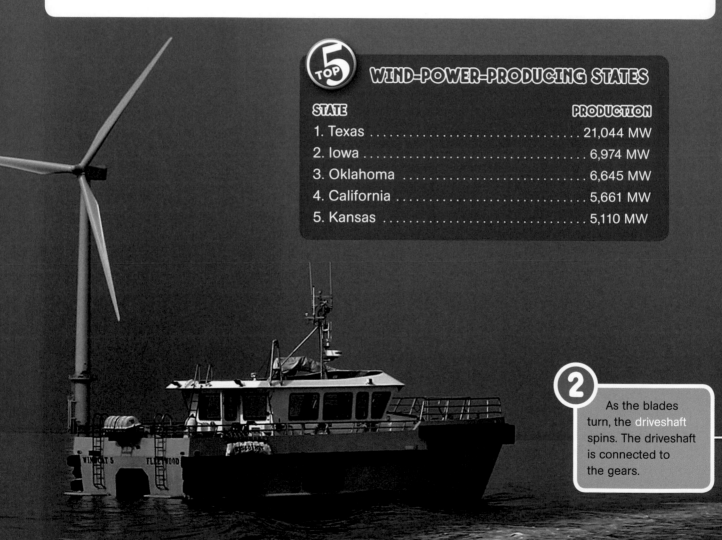

TOP 5 WIND-POWER-PRODUCING STATES

STATE	PRODUCTION
1. Texas	21,044 MW
2. Iowa	6,974 MW
3. Oklahoma	6,645 MW
4. California	5,661 MW
5. Kansas	5,110 MW

2 As the blades turn, the driveshaft spins. The driveshaft is connected to the gears.

Fast Fact

Wind turbines are built tall to catch winds that often blow high above the ground. Most are as tall as a 20-story building, while some are twice as high.

The casing holds the driveshaft, gears, and a generator.

ILL WINDS?

Not everyone loves wind power. Some people complain that the huge machines make the landscape ugly. Wind turbines also make a steady noise, which can be bothersome. Many environmentalists oppose wind turbines because the spinning blades can kill birds and bats.

Those in favor of wind turbines say their benefits are far greater than their drawbacks. Wind turbines are a clean source of energy and reduce the use of polluting fossil fuels, such as coal, oil, and gas.

1 Wind makes the lightweight blades turn. The faster the blades spin, the more electricity is produced. The blades are connected to the driveshaft.

3 The driveshaft turns gears, which make another driveshaft spin even faster. This driveshaft leads to a generator.

4 The generator converts the spin of the driveshaft into an electrical current.

5 Electricity from the generator flows down wires to a transformer. This device makes the current stronger. The electricity is sent through power lines to homes and towns.

157

HOW can schools use the sun's energy?

The sun is the biggest source of energy in the solar system. The sun's energy can even be used to run a computer, power a science lab, and light an entire building! Thanks to solar panels, solar energy can be converted into electricity to power these activities. School districts around the country are increasingly "going green," converting existing power systems to solar ones—and even building solar schools from scratch.

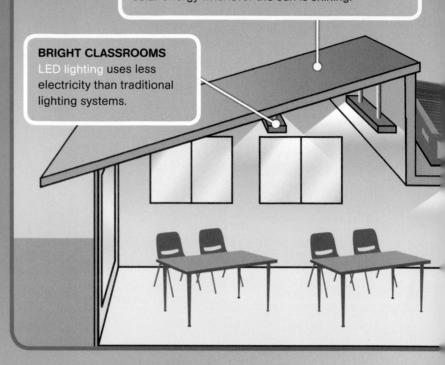

UP ON THE ROOF Most schools are built with flat roofs, which provide plenty of open space for installing solar panels. The wide, flat roofs are unshaded, so solar panels placed there can collect solar energy whenever the sun is shining.

BRIGHT CLASSROOMS LED lighting uses less electricity than traditional lighting systems.

GREEN SCHOOL

In 2012, Green School in Bali, Indonesia, was named the greenest school on Earth by the Center for Green Schools at the U.S. Green Building Council. More than 100 solar panels provide 80% of the energy the school needs. The school buildings are built with sustainable materials. Opened in 2008 with 90 students, Green School now has 400 students from more than 30 countries.

PRESTO CHANGO!

Solar cells generate a type of electricity called direct current (DC); buildings use a type of electricity called alternating current (AC). A device known as an inverter changes DC to AC so that a building can use the electricity its solar cells have created. Wires connect an inverter to an electrical panel, or breaker box. All the energy generated by solar panels funnels through this box.

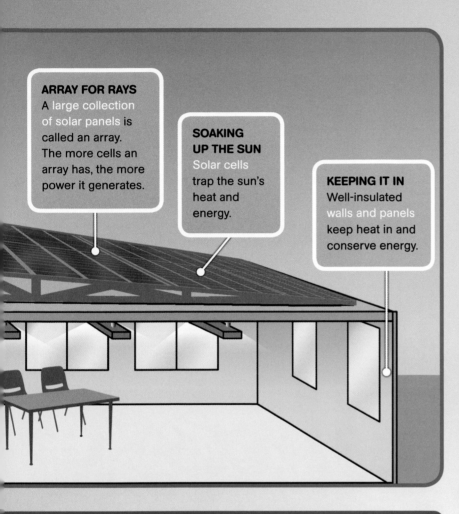

ARRAY FOR RAYS
A large collection of solar panels is called an array. The more cells an array has, the more power it generates.

SOAKING UP THE SUN
Solar cells trap the sun's heat and energy.

KEEPING IT IN
Well-insulated walls and panels keep heat in and conserve energy.

SOLAR CELLS are the key to solar power systems. The cells are thin devices made of silicon and other materials. Individual solar cells are combined into sheets called solar panels, which are placed where they will catch as much sunlight as possible. The rays of the sun hit the cells, and a chemical reaction sends out electrons. The solar cells convert those electrons into electrical energy. This reaction is called the photoelectric or photovoltaic effect, which is why solar cells are sometimes called PV cells.

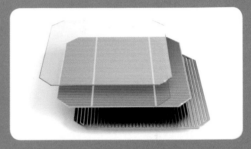

SOLAR HEAT can heat water, too. The hot water is stored in a tank connected to the building's plumbing.

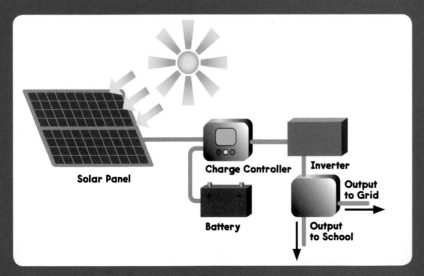

Solar Panel

Charge Controller

Battery

Inverter

Output to Grid

Output to School

HOW are computers and other electronics recycled?

Many people know how to recycle plastic, glass, metal, and paper products. But how do we get rid of computers, cell phones, TVs, and other electronic devices that we don't want?

One solution is to give away usable electronics to schools, charities, and other groups. If a device can't be reused, it can be recycled.

See how a large recycling plant takes gadgets apart and puts some back together.

1 Every day, recycling plants receive electronic waste (e-waste), including cell phones, computers, cameras, and printers.

5 E-waste that workers can't break apart is fed into machines that separate out pieces made of different materials, such as copper. Many electronics contain small amounts of valuable metals, such as gold, which are removed and sold. Dangerous materials, such as lead, are also removed and sent to special landfills and waste plants.

Fast Fact
About 7,500 pounds of gold can be recovered from 100 million recycled cell phones.

2 Workers stack discarded computers, which will be stripped of their parts.

3 The workers take computers and other gadgets apart. They sort the pieces according to the material they are made of. As many of the parts as possible are recycled—from plastic wrapping to broken glass and metal scraps. These are sold to separate recycling factories.

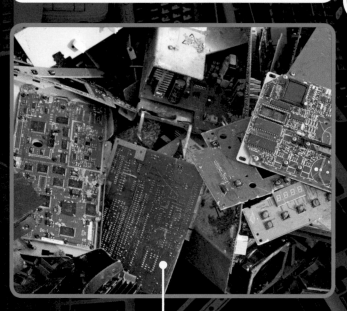

4 Much e-waste contains parts, such as circuits, that will be sold to manufacturers and used again in new products or in rebuilt devices.

Did You Know?

E-waste can contain harmful toxins such as lead, mercury, cadmium, and arsenic. Recycling can make a difference—e-waste makes up 70% of toxic waste, but at present just 12.5% of all e-waste is recycled.

HOW do you stay safe in a hurricane?

Hurricanes are huge storms that begin over warm ocean waters. They can last more than a week, travel hundreds of miles, and stretch 500 miles wide. States along the Gulf of Mexico and the East Coast of the U.S. are often the hardest hit.

Hurricane winds can reach 160 mph, flinging objects and shattering glass. The most dangerous part of a hurricane is the storm surge, which happens when powerful winds push ocean water onto the shore, causing floods. Storm surges account for most of a hurricane's damage. Preparedness is the key to staying safe.

Fortunately, modern tools allow meteorologists to track and predict the path of storms, giving people time to move to safety. If officials recommend evacuation, leaving the area is always the safest course. But there are many things you can do to ride out less powerful storms, and to protect your home if you have to leave it.

Before a Hurricane Strikes

✹ Make plans to keep your home and property safe. Close storm shutters or cover windows with plywood. Tape won't keep windows from breaking.

✹ Listen to the radio or TV for information.

✹ Bring outdoor furniture and other objects indoors.

✹ Turn off gas and electricity if told to by officials.

✹ Only use the phone for emergencies.

✹ Be sure there is a supply of food to eat and water for drinking and flushing toilets.

✹ Leave your home if ordered to by local authorities. Follow their instructions.

✹ If you live in a building with many stories, go to the lowest level. Hurricane winds are stronger at higher levels.

✹ If you live on a coast, or in an area near water, and can't escape the storm:

- Stay indoors during the hurricane and away from windows and glass doors.
- Close all doors inside and outside your home.
- Stay in a small inner room, closet, or hallway on the lowest level.
- Lie on the floor under a table or another strong object.

After the Storm

* Don't return to a home that was damaged by floodwater before local officials declare the area safe.

* Use a phone only to report emergencies.

* Stay off the streets. There can be electrical wires on the ground, as well as weakened walls, bridges, roads, and sidewalks.

* Don't enter a home without an adult. An adult should make sure there are no loose power lines, gas leaks, or damage to the structure of the building.

* Enter the home carefully and check for damage. Be careful of loose boards and slippery floors.

* Never eat food touched by floodwater.

HOW TO BUILD A HURRICANE-PROOF HOME

Here's what specialists may do in some high-risk hurricane areas:

SHUTTERED WINDOWS Cut plywood ahead of time, and snap PlyLox window clips into place when a hurricane is approaching. The clips dig into the window casing and hold the shutters tight in winds up to 150 mph.

FULL-STRENGTH GARAGE DOORS Garage doors are the weakest point in a home during a storm. Once they are torn off, high winds can enter a house. Metal braces anchor the doors to the wall and the floor, making it possible for the doors to withstand 180-mph winds.

SECURED ROOF Simple steel clips drilled into the roof trusses and wall beams can keep the roof in place during a storm.

MISSILE-PROOF DOORS Flying debris can become missiles that pierce walls and doors during a storm. Safety doors have polyurethane-wrapped steel at the center, so they don't splinter.

HOW do volunteers clean up the oceans?

Wood, food, and even most metals biodegrade, or break down, over time. During biodegradation, bacteria transform the materials into useful matter, such as compost. Plastic, however, never biodegrades. Every piece of plastic that has been created still exists, and many of them are turning our oceans into a plastic-filled soup.

Volunteers work together to clean up a beach in Hawaii.

ON THE BEACH Approximately 5.3 trillion pieces of plastic, weighing nearly 270,000 tons, float on the surface of the oceans. You might recognize some of this trash, like action figures and toothbrushes. Most of it, though, is just tiny plastic scraps no bigger than dimes. Currents and tides bring it to beaches all over the world, where volunteers help collect it.

WHY IT MATTERS Animals—including fish, birds, and whales—sometimes mistake plastic for food and are harmed or die when they eat it. Sea turtles eat jellyfish, and floating plastic bags look just like jellies to them.

HOW YOU CAN HELP

The Ocean Conservancy's International Coastal Cleanup recruits thousands of volunteers annually to clean up our plastic mess. In the past 30 years, more than 9 million volunteers have collected nearly 164 million pounds of trash. If you live near water, you can organize a cleanup, too. Cleaning up rivers and streams means trash there won't end up in the ocean.

Pick a location. Take a parent with you to scout out a beach area that is safe and in need of cleaning. Contact the local government for permission to clean there.

Gather volunteers. Recruit friends, neighbors, classmates, Scout groups . . . and any other willing helpers.

Come prepared. Volunteers will need hats, sunscreen, water, gloves, and sturdy, closed-toe shoes.

Get supplies. Have enough trash bags and trash pickers on hand.

Safety first! An adult with first aid certification (and first aid kit) should always be present.

Check in. Supply a sign-in sheet and pens. This way you can let volunteers know next time you organize a cleanup.

Start cleaning. Work in teams to collect trash and fill out data cards with the information you gather. Researchers analyze data on these cards to find ways to lessen the impact of ocean pollution.

To find data cards and more information, go to *oceanconservancy.org/trash-free-seas/ international-coastal-cleanup/start-a-cleanup/.*

WATER WORRIES

Much of the world's floating trash ends up in one of five major gyres, or swirling patterns, in the oceans. Ocean currents carry trash and deposit it in the calm centers of the gyres. The Great Pacific Garbage Patch includes the Western Garbage Patch, located near Japan, and the Eastern Garbage Patch, which sits between Hawaii and California. Boyan Slat, a young inventor, is creating a 65-mile-wide trash collection initiative called the Ocean Cleanup. Some believe Ocean Cleanup could reduce trash in the Great Pacific Garbage Patch by 50% in just five years.

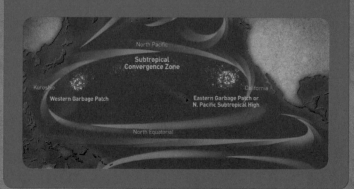

North Pacific

Subtropical
Convergence Zone

Kuroshio

California

Western Garbage Patch

Eastern Garbage Patch or
N. Pacific Subtropical High

North Equatorial

HOW TO campaign for a cause

In a free democracy, citizens have the right to make their voices heard. Doing that can take the form of working to change laws, bringing greater awareness to an issue that affects a community, or raising funds to support a favorite charity. We all have causes we are passionate about, and we all have the power to bring about change. Even small actions can make a big difference. Here's how to get started.

What to do:

2 DO RESEARCH Use the Internet and the library to learn more about your cause. Find nonprofit groups that are already working for change. Research government agencies that have produced reports on the topic. Talk to your parents, too. Knowing your subject well will help you know how you can best help.

3 FORM A COMMITTEE It's time to raise awareness and get people to join your cause. Invite classmates and friends to a meeting to discuss your course of action. Perhaps the best solution is to organize an activity or volunteer for an existing organization. Put your heads together and agree on the best way forward.

1 IDENTIFY A PROBLEM What problems do people face at your school or in your community? Are you concerned about the environment? Are you an animal rights activist? Do you want to help stop bullying? Would you like to support research for a particular disease? Narrow your focus to just one problem, then jump in.

THINK LOCAL Supporting things you care about can mean taking action when it matters. Middle-school students in Old Orchard Beach, Maine, led the way in this demonstration against school budget cuts. You can make a difference close to home. A cause you care about can often be found in your own community. Look around and see how you can help make the world a better place.

4 HOLD A FUND-RAISER Plan a Saturday morning bake sale or sign up for a fund-raising walk. A parent can help spread the word through e-mail and social media. Parents can also consider helping to donate supplies, cook, or sponsor you for a walk. Send the proceeds to your chosen charity.

6 START A PETITION OR A LETTER-WRITING CAMPAIGN If your cause involves changing local, state, or even national laws, the pen can be a mighty tool. Find out who the decision-makers are and write, write, write. Start a petition and collect signatures to show officials how much support there is for your cause. Or your committee can write letters urging change.

5 ORGANIZE A COMMUNITY ACTIVITY Designate a day on which students and volunteers clean up a local park, pick up trash from around your school or a nearby park, or plant trees and shrubs on school grounds. Enlist the help of parents and teachers in gaining permission and permits to do so.

7 ATTEND A RALLY People come together to rally for their causes and make their opinions clear. Peaceful rallies and protests can be effective change agents. Attend a rally with your family and friends. Share your experiences.

CHAPTER 11

JUST FOR FUN

HOW does an idea become a book?

Ideas for books come from many people. Experienced writers, editors (who select texts to publish, and make changes and corrections), agents (who connect writers and editors), and those outside the publishing business can all generate ideas. Even if someone has never published a book before, he or she can pitch an idea to an agent or editor, who may agree to help develop it.

A book idea can start with a phrase, a title, a person you know or are interested in, a historical event, or an experience you've had. Do you have a book idea? Is your idea for a nonfiction book, which could be based on a true story, a real person or thing, or a historical event? Or is it fiction—a made-up story?

1 **WHAT'S THE STORY?** Once you've figured out what you want to write about, it's time to think about what your book will look like. Will it be a chapter book, a picture book, or perhaps an information book about animals that live in the ocean? Where will the story be set? Will the action happen in a single day or over time? These are the sorts of things a writer needs to figure out when turning an idea into a manuscript.

Fast Fact

Making a book is a collaborative effort—it requires the skills of many people. In addition to a writer, an editor, and a designer, a book needs a project manager to assign deadlines and keep team members on track.

4 **DESIGNING AND MANUFACTURING** Once the manuscript is ready, a copyeditor corrects punctuation and grammar mistakes. Then off the text goes to a designer, who turns an ordinary typed document into pages with art, using special computer programs for graphic design. A proofreader checks the designed pages for errors. Then an electronic file is dispatched to a printer. And—presto! A physical book is born.

All work and no fun is . . . well . . . no fun. Catch the fun fever and become a top domino toppler. Get the lowdown on how videos are made, how fireworks light the skies, and how balloons become animals.

2 **WRITING IT** The next step is to create a manuscript—the text of the book. Usually the writer will start by creating an outline. Then the writer will compose the sentences, reviewing over and over and making rewrites. If a writer is able to interest an editor in a manuscript, then the writer and editor work as a team to ensure the book contains the right information for the intended audience.

3 **EDITING** The writer shares the work in progress with the editor, who provides feedback. The editor may change some language to make it clearer, verify facts, and offer suggestions about how to tell the story. Revision and rewriting are key: the manuscript goes back and forth between writer and editor several times.

As the *HMS Scout* dove deep, Cam saw something amazing.

It was gray.

It was BIG.

It was a humpback whale!

HOW is a fireworks show staged?

The Fourth of July isn't the same without a fireworks display. The experts who put on these shows are called pyrotechnicians (pi-roh-tek-*nish*-unz). They build and shoot off the fireworks. To create a spectacular show, pyrotechnicians must figure out what types of fireworks should go off—and in what order. They must think about the colors, sounds, heights, and patterns of the fireworks. In some shows, the fireworks must match up with music. Pyrotechnicians are the only people legally allowed to handle fireworks in most states. Leave fireworks to the experts, and enjoy the show! Here is how a professional fireworks show is put on.

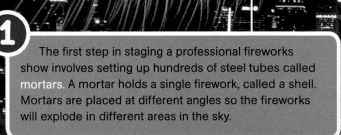

1 The first step in staging a professional fireworks show involves setting up hundreds of steel tubes called mortars. A mortar holds a single firework, called a shell. Mortars are placed at different angles so the fireworks will explode in different areas in the sky.

2 A pyrotechnician places a shell in each mortar. At the bottom of the shell is gunpowder. When the powder explodes, it sends the shell into the sky.

IT'S A BLAST!

An aerial firework is a firework that explodes high in the air. To build one, an expert places a fuse in a shell, or paper tube. The shell is packed with black powder, as well as chemicals formed into little balls or cubes, called stars. It's the stars that give the fireworks their colors and patterns in the sky. Finally, the shell is wrapped in thick paper hardened by paste and shaped into a cylinder or sphere.

Fuse

Black powder

Stars

Shell

When a firework is lit, black powder in the bottom of the shell rockets it out of a mortar and into the sky. As the firework rises, the fuse inside the shell burns down. When the shell reaches its peak, the fuse lights the black powder in the shell. The exploding powder makes the stars burn in a shower of colorful sparks.

3 Before the show, workers begin to connect the fireworks to a firing panel with wires. The firing panel sits far from the mortars.

4 The fireworks are set off far enough away from spectators so pieces of the exploding shells won't land on the crowds. At a July Fourth fireworks display in New York City, they were set off from a barge in the middle of a river.

5 At the press of a button, an electric current ignites the powder in a mortar. One by one, the fireworks blast 300 to 600 feet into the sky and burst into colors. The final fireworks, the finale, is loud and spectacular. The crowds applaud.

HOW do you lay out and topple dominoes?

Dominoes topple like . . . well . . . dominoes. Knock over the one at the head of the line, and it sets in motion a chain reaction—sometimes a very *loooong* chain reaction. In 2009, one display in the Netherlands toppled 4.5 million dominoes!

So how can you create one of these elaborate constructions? The pro advice is to start simple. Set up a short, straight line of dominoes—each about half an inch apart—to get the hang of the process. Bring lots of patience: it can be frustrating if one domino falls before they're all in place and you have to start again from scratch.

Did You Know?

In April 2017, the California state domino toppling record was broken at the San Jose Children's Discovery Museum when high school students set up and toppled 25,000 dominoes.

Tenth Annual Domino Toppling Extravaganza (Brattleboro Museum & Art Center, 2017)

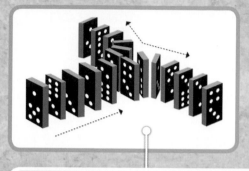

SPLITS A split is where the last domino in a line topples two side-by-side tiles, which in turn knock down two separate lines.

DIAMONDS With an initial split, it's possible to form a diamond pattern.

CURVES Form a curved line by placing tiles at a slight angle—a 30-degree angle is good—to the left or right.

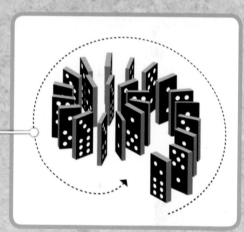

SPIRALS Anything but basic, domino spirals use the same technique you use to make curves.

RAMPS Another trick to incorporate is a ramp—but be careful it isn't too steep, or the tiles won't fall neatly.

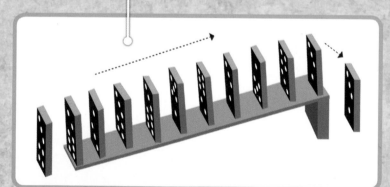

PRO TIP When setting up a large display, leave a number of wide gaps between the tiles at intervals. That way, if you accidentally knock over a tile, the entire display won't come crashing down. Once the display is complete, fill in the gaps before setting the dominoes in motion.

HOW does a new word get into the dictionary?

Dictionaries are books of words. The words are generally listed in alphabetical order, from *A* to *Z*. Each word's entry includes a definition, which explains what the word means and how it's used. While English-language dictionaries have been around for more than 400 years, they haven't always included the same words. Here's a look at how new words are added to a dictionary.

FIRST Dictionary editors read a lot to find new words. They read books, magazines, newspapers, and online materials. They use computers to track how often new words are used and over what period of time. Editors also look for new uses or spellings of existing words. They mark words that are used often and in interesting ways.

NEXT Marked words may be tracked on index cards, by computer, or both. Each word's record includes examples of usage and information about where it has been used. This record is called a citation. Citation databases may contain millions of words that are being tracked.

THEN Editors review citations regularly. They determine whether a marked word has been used enough, if it adds enough new meaning to the language, and whether it should be considered for entry into the dictionary. They also decide whether a word has faded from use and should be dropped from the citation database.

FINALLY The *Oxford English Dictionary (OED)*, first published in 1884, contains more than 600,000 words today. Every three months, editors update the dictionary. In September 2016, they added more than 500 new words. Here are a few of those new words, along with their definitions and an example sentence for each.

TFK SPECIAL REPORT

card reader
noun
1. an electronic device that reads a magnetic strip or bar code on a credit, debit, or identity card

Before her groceries were bagged, Priya swiped her card through the card reader.

YOLO
interjection
1. "You only live once"; used to express the view that one should make the most of the present moment without worrying about the future (often as a rationale for impulsive or reckless behavior)

   As Hannah parachuted out of the plane, she yelled, "YOLO!"

Here's why you should own a print or digital dictionary:

* To look up unfamiliar words you come across in books, in articles, and online.

* To help with spelling when you're doing homework or playing word games with friends.

* To build your vocabulary by increasing the number of words you know and use.

* To figure out which spelling to use when two words sound alike, such as *principal* (the head of a school) and *principle* (a rule or belief).

PARTS OF SPEECH
Noun A person, place, or thing: *teacher, carrot, friendship*. It may be preceded by an article (*the, a, an*).

Pronoun Takes the place of a noun: *you, they, it.*

Verb Expresses an action or a state of being: *to jump, to love.*

Adjective Describes a noun: *good, hot, blue.*

Adverb Modifies (adds to or changes) the meaning of a verb, telling something like where, when, how, or how much: *outside, later, slowly, very.*

Preposition Shows how something is related to the rest of a sentence: *by, about, with.*

Conjunction Joins words, phrases, or parts of sentences: *and, but, or.*

Interjection Expresses emotion: *Wow! Ugh! Ouch!*

cheer squad
noun
1. a team of cheerleaders

   The cheer squad posed for a team picture.

scrumdiddlyumptious
adjective
1. extremely scrumptious; excellent, splendid; (esp. of food) delicious

   The juicy watermelon is scrumdiddlyumptious.

HOW do roller coasters go up and down?

A roller coaster is like a scary movie: it gives riders thrills and chills without putting them in danger. How do these scream machines move people up, down, and around? It takes energy. As a roller coaster car is pulled up the first hill, it stores potential energy. The higher it goes, the more potential energy it has. When gravity pulls the coaster down the track, the coaster releases the potential energy. Now it has kinetic energy, which is the energy an object has when it moves. The faster an object moves, the more kinetic energy it has. The coaster is moving fastest after it goes down the first and highest hill. This gives the car enough energy to go up the next hill.

A coaster can't go up and down hills forever. Air resistance and the friction of the wheels against the track make the car lose energy and eventually slow down. That's why each hill is smaller and smaller.

2 Motorized chains pull the cars up the first hill. Some rides use magnets in the cars and track to pull the cars quickly up the first hill.

3 The first hill is the highest. The coaster gains enough kinetic energy going down this first hill to go up the next hill.

1 Safety bars and heavy seat belts keep riders inside the car.

4 The second hill is next highest. At the bottom of the second hill, the coaster has just enough energy to reach the top of the third hill.

TOP 5 HIGHEST ROLLER COASTERS IN THE WORLD

COASTER	HEIGHT (FEET)	AMUSEMENT PARK	LOCATION
1. Kingda Ka	456	Six Flags Great Adventure	Jackson, New Jersey
2. Top Thrill Dragster	420	Cedar Point	Sandusky, Ohio
3. Superman: Escape from Krypton	415	Six Flags Magic Mountain	Valencia, California
4. Tower of Terror II	377	Dreamworld	Coomera, Australia
5. Red Force	367.4	PortAventura Park	Salou, Spain

If you're looking for the world's fastest roller coaster, you'll have to travel to Abu Dhabi, in the United Arab Emirates. The Formula Rossa coaster at the Ferrari World amusement park can reach a top speed of 149 miles per hour! It doesn't waste any time, either, hitting 60 miles per hour within a mere two seconds of launching.

5 Three sets of car wheels run above, under, and alongside the track. They keep the cars locked when they make twists, turns, and loop-de-loops.

Riders on a loop-de-loop don't fall out thanks to centrifugal (cen-*trif*-uh-gull) force. The force of the cars moving in a circle pushes riders back toward the floor of the cars. It's the same as when you whirl a bucket of water in a big circle around your head. The water stays in the bucket!

HOW is a short online video produced?

Online video production involves many people with different skills working as a team. And like making a movie or television show, video production is broken down into specific steps. Producing even a short online video can be a lengthy task, and having a set work pattern makes the process flow smoothly. It also helps avoid the costly process of having to do it a second time. Preproduction, production, and postproduction are the three steps in making a video.

Did You Know?

Using a series of drawings called storyboards, based on a script, filmmakers map out each shot they will take before they film. The process helps them figure out how to set up shots, where to make edits, and how to order the action. Good storyboarding saves time during production and postproduction.

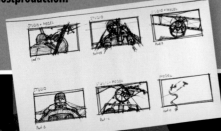

POPULAR ONLINE VIDEO CATEGORIES Online videos run the gambit from video blogs (vlogs) to cooking shows, to silly skits. But some categories are more popular than others. These are the four most popular types:

NEWS

COMEDY

HOW TO

MUSIC

TOP 5 MOST POPULAR YOUTUBE VIDEOS OF 2016

VIDEO	VIEWS (MILLIONS)
1. Carpool Karaoke with Adele	135.8
2. Pen-Pineapple-Apple-Pen/PIKO-TARO	95
3. What's Inside a Rattlesnake Rattle?	59.5
4. Nike Football Presents: The Switch Featuring Cristiano Ronaldo	57
5. Grace VanderWaal: 12-Year-Old Ukulele Player Gets Golden Buzzer	46.4

VIDEO 101 Whether you're making a blockbuster action movie or a lip-sync video to post online, there are basic steps to follow before, during, and after filming.

PREPRODUCTION Preproduction is everything that needs to happen before the cameras start rolling: coming up with a concept for the video, writing a script, and assembling the equipment. Many small and often unpredictable details are involved—for instance, scouting for places to set the action and acquiring the necessary filming permits.

PRODUCTION Production is the actual shooting, or filming, of the video. Most video content today is shot on digital cameras, or even digital devices such as smartphones or laptop webcams. The type of camera used depends on the size and budget of the shoot. A webcam may be sufficient for someone creating a simple instructional YouTube video. More involved shoots, however, may require digital camcorders with built-in audio, special zoom lenses, and other advanced features.

POSTPRODUCTION Once shooting is complete, it's time for postproduction. The video editor selects clips, or shots, from the footage and edits them together so they tell the desired story. The editor also ensures that the dialogue (talking) and images are in sync. Often sound effects, music, voiceover narration, and graphics are added. Once it's completed, it's time to encode the video so it can be played on sites like YouTube.

GETTING THE WORD OUT Sometimes an online video goes viral, which means it's shared rapidly through social media. Search engine optimization (SEO) is important. It helps search engines such as Google find something specific. For example, if the video is about sea otters being utterly adorable, using SEO tools can help ensure that the video turns up when someone searches "cute animals."

HOW TO
make a balloon animal

Remember to ask an adult for help.

Becoming a master balloon twister takes lots of practice, but almost anyone with a little patience and dexterity can quickly grasp the basics. Step one is to inflate a balloon, but only partially. Then tie it off. Twisters leave balloons partly inflated so they can shape them without popping them.

Once the balloon is tied off, the twister uses a combination of techniques to create an animal. The basic twist involves rotating the balloon to create two separate segments. The lock twist puts two basic twists around each other so they "lock" into place. For a loop or fold twist, a long, thin balloon is folded in half and the two ends are twisted together to form a loop.

Professional twisters use what are called 260 balloons, which are designed for twisting. Their pencil-like shape makes them easy to manipulate. The 260 means that, when inflated, each balloon is two inches in diameter and 60 inches long.

What you need:

- A long, thin 260 balloon
- A handheld air pump (optional, but easier for blowing up the balloon)

What to do:

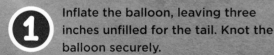

1 Inflate the balloon, leaving three inches unfilled for the tail. Knot the balloon securely.

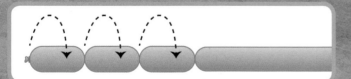

2 Use basic twists to create four segments: the first segment for the dog's nose, the second and third for its ears, and the fourth for its body.

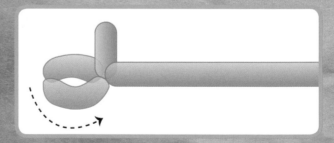

3 Twist the second and third segments together in a lock twist to form a nose and ears.

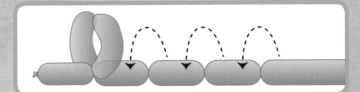

WARNING Balloons can pose a choking hazard to babies and toddlers. Always keep balloons away from very young children.

4 Twist a few inches below the head to make the dog's neck. Make two more segments below the neck for the legs. Twist the legs together in a lock twist.

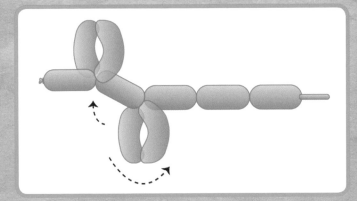

5 Twist the remainder of the body three times to make four segments. The first will be the body, the second and third the back legs, and the last the tail.

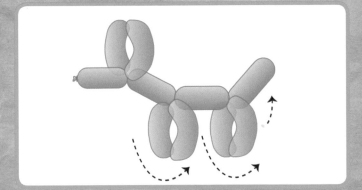

6 Fold the balloon at the twist between the two leg segments. Hold them together and twist them around the end of the body segment. The tail will then fill up. Doggie done!

More fun!

Balloon artists often specialize in either single-balloon models (designs made with just one balloon) or multiple-balloon models (which are made of many connecting balloons). With multiple balloons, they can create almost anything.

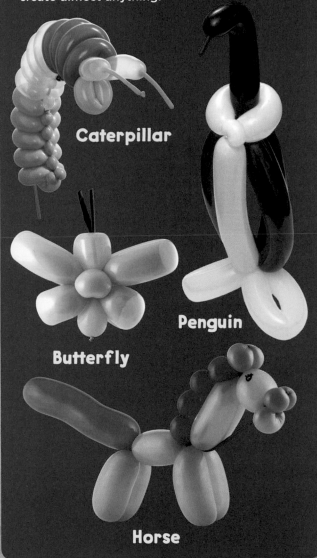

Caterpillar

Penguin

Butterfly

Horse

Glossary

A

actin A protein found in muscle filaments, needed for muscle contraction.

actuator A mechanical device that controls movement.

airfoil A wing or propeller blade on an airplane or helicopter that provides force when in motion.

Antarctica The ice-covered continent around the South Pole.

antenna 1. One of two sensory organs on the head of an insect. The plural of *antenna* is *antennae*.
2. A metal device used for sending and receiving radio waves.

antibiotic A medicine that kills bacteria.

app A computer program that performs a certain function. *App* is short for *application*.

arachnid A type of arthropod (an animal without a backbone) that has two body sections and eight legs and usually lives on land. Spiders, scorpions, and ticks are arachnids.

Arctic The area around the North Pole.

asteroid A rock that orbits the sun, especially between Mars and Jupiter. An asteroid can be the size of a small planet.

astigmatism The inability of the eye to focus light because the cornea doesn't curve normally.

autotroph An organism that can create its own source of energy.

auxiliary memory Secondary storage on a computer, which does not lose stored data when the computer is turned off. ROM is auxiliary memory.

B

bacteria Microscopic single-celled organisms found in water, air, and soil.

battery A device that produces electrical current.

binary Made up of two things.

biodegrade Broken down into harmless products, especially by microorganisms.

bioluminescence The emission of light from an organism.

blubber A thick layer of fat found in a marine animal that insulates, or protects, it from the cold.

buoyancy The ability of an object to float or to rise when submerged in a liquid.

burr The rough, prickly seed case of a plant.

bycatch Unintended capture of fish and other marine animals while fishing.

C

caisson A watertight chamber used during construction work in water.

calve To break off, as when an iceberg calves from a glacier.

canal A human-made waterway used for travel, to ship goods, or to irrigate land.

canyon A deep valley with steep sides, often formed by a river.

cell 1. The basic structure of every living thing.
2. A geographic area that is part of a cellular telephone system; another name for a mobile phone.
3. The basic unit of a solar cell system; together, solar cells make up a solar array, which generates energy.

centrifugal force The force directed away from the center of a revolving body.

cephalopod A type of animal that has a soft body, usually a hard shell, and multiple arms or tentacles. It lives in water and usually can squirt ink in self-defense. Squid and octopuses are cephalopods.

chaff The seed coverings thrown away during the harvesting of grain.

chloroplast The part of a plant cell where photosynthesis takes place.

chrysalis The protective layer covering an insect pupa.

chyme Food that has been turned into a liquidlike mass in the stomach.

comet A large chunk of rock surrounded by frozen gas and ice that orbits the sun.

cone A cell in the retina of the eye that detects color.

cornea The clear area that covers the front of the eye and focuses light.

crustacean A large class of mostly water-dwelling animals that have a hard exoskeleton. Lobsters, shrimp, and crabs are crustaceans.

D

derailleur A device on a bicycle that shifts gears by moving a chain from one gear wheel to another. *Derailleur* comes from the French for "to derail."

displacement The volume of water moved out of position by a ship.

dissolve To add a solid substance to a liquid so that the solid and the liquid form a uniform mixture.

E

e-waste Electronic waste, such as computers or cell phones that have been thrown away.

ecosystem A complex group of organisms that function as a unit.

electromagnetic field A magnetic field produced when electricity flows through a wire.

electron A tiny particle charged with negative electricity that moves around the nucleus of an atom.

electroreceptor A special sensory organ in sharks and some other fish that detects electricity given off by other sea creatures.

endangered In immediate danger of becoming extinct, or dying out completely.

entomologist A scientist who studies insects.

esophagus The tube that passes food from the mouth to the stomach.

exoplanet A planet outside our solar system.

extinct No longer in existence.

F

farsighted Unable to see close objects clearly.

fixie A fixed-gear bicycle.

fossil Part of a plant or animal from the distant past that has been preserved in the Earth's crust.

fusion The combining of atomic nuclei to create heavier nuclei. This process generates energy.

G

gear A wheel with teeth that turns another wheel with teeth, so the motion of one controls the speed of the other.

glacier A large mass of ice and snow, pressed down over thousands of years, that slowly moves forward.

gland A cell or group of cells that produces a substance that the body uses or gets rid of.

gravity The force of attraction between two objects.

grommet A sturdy ring used to protect an opening.

H

hurricane A storm that forms over tropical waters with winds that reach at least 74 miles per hour.

hybrid Something that combines two or more different things, such as a car that runs on both electricity and gas.

I

iceberg A large chunk of ice that breaks off from a glacier or an ice shelf and floats in the water.

immune system The cells, proteins, and tissues that protect the body from infection and disease.

infection The invasion of the body by a microorganism that causes disease, such as a virus.

inflammation Pain, swelling, and redness in the body, caused by infection or injury.

infrared Using or making rays of light that are not visible at the red end of the light spectrum.

invertebrate An animal without a backbone.

J

joint A part of the body where two bones are connected.

K

kinetic energy The energy of movement.

L

landfill A site designed so large amounts of trash can be buried there safely.

larva The earliest stage of an insect or animal, just after it has hatched and before it changes into an adult.

LED A semiconductor device that emits light when an electric current passes through it. *LED* stands for *light-emitting diode*.

lens The part of the eye that helps bring rays of light into focus.

lift The aerodynamic force that acts on an airplane and causes it to rise.

ligament A tough tissue that connects two bones.

limestone A kind of rock often used as a building material.

lock 1. A large chamber with gates at each end that fills with water to raise ships as they pass through it, or drains to lower them.

2. A device that secures a door or container and can be opened with a key or combination.

luciferase A protein that causes luciferin to activate.

luciferin The substance within a luminescent organism that causes it to produce light.

lymphocyte A type of white blood cell that helps confer immunity.

M

macrophage A type of large phagocyte in the immune system.

magnet An object that attracts certain kinds of metal, such as iron and nickel.

magnetic field The area around a magnetic substance where its magnetic forces can be observed.

magnetic levitation The process by which an object, such as a train, is suspended by magnetic fields. *Magnetic levitation* is shortened to *maglev*.

main memory Primary storage on a computer, which loses data when the computer is turned off. RAM is main memory.

mammal A type of warm-blooded animal that has hair or fur and a backbone and feeds milk to its young.

mass The quantity of matter in an object.

mass extinction An extinction caused by a widespread disaster that kills off many species of living things in a fairly short period of time.

megawatt A unit of electrical power, equal to 1 million watts.

melanin The pigment that gives hair or skin its color.

membrane A thin layer of tissue that covers, separates, or connects areas of the body.

metamorphosis The series of physical changes that an animal such as a butterfly undergoes after birth or hatching.

microbe A germ.

microwave A type of electromagnetic radiation, similar to a radio wave. Microwaves are used in microwave ovens to cook food.

mineral A substance that occurs naturally and is found in rocks, soil, and bones.

molecule The smallest part of a substance that still contains all the substance's properties.

molt To shed hair, feathers, or another outside covering.

motherboard The main circuit board of a computer.

mucus A thick fluid that coats and protects the nose, the throat, the lungs, and other areas of the body.

myosin A protein in muscles that reacts with actin during muscle contraction.

N

nearsighted Unable to see distant objects clearly.

nebula A cloud of stars or gas and dust in space.

nectar The sweet liquid created by a plant that attracts insects or birds, causing them to pollinate the plant.

nocturnal Active at night.

nymph An immature insect.

O

orbit The path one body takes around another, such as the path of the Earth around the sun.

orthodontist A dentist who specializes in correcting crooked teeth.

osteoblast A type of cell that rebuilds bone.

osteoclast A type of cell that dissolves bone.

P

paleontologist A scientist who studies fossils of prehistoric organisms.

pepsin A chemical produced in the stomach that helps break down proteins for digestion.

phagocyte A type of cell that protects the body by absorbing foreign material and debris. Macrophages and microphages are phagocytes.

phloem A tissue that contains the tubes that carry food throughout a plant.

photon A small particle of energy that all forms of electromagnetic radiation are made of.

photophore A light-emitting organ seen mostly on deep-sea fish.

photosynthesis The process by which plants make their own energy from carbon dioxide and hydrogen.

pigment The substance in plants and animals that gives cells color.

plaster A powder that becomes a paste when mixed with water and hardens as it dries.

platelet A flat disk in the blood that helps the blood clot.

pollution The contamination of air, water, or soil by harmful substances.

predator An animal that hunts and eats other animals.

prey An animal that is hunted and eaten by another animal.

primate A type of mammal that has a large brain and five digits on each hand and foot. Monkeys, apes, and humans are primates.

protein A substance basic to living cells and necessary for an organism to function. Protein is an important source of energy in a person's diet.

pupa The stage in the development of certain insects that comes after the larva stage and before the adult stage. A pupa often changes into an adult while inside a cocoon or a hard outer layer.

pupil The opening in the center of the eye through which light enters.

pyrotechnician An expert in the use of fireworks.

Q

quarry An open area from which rock used for building things, such as limestone, is removed.

R

radiation Electromagnetic energy that moves in the form of waves.

recycle To collect materials, such as metal cans and glass bottles, that have been thrown away in order to reuse them in new products.

refrigerant A substance used in a refrigerator or air conditioner that lowers temperatures by absorbing heat.

retina The light-sensitive tissue located at the back of the eyeball.

rod A cell in the retina of the eye that is sensitive to black-and-white light.

S

seed The part of a plant that can grow into a new plant.

social media The different forms of electronic communication, such as websites for social networking, that allow users to create online communities.

solar panel A device made up of solar cells, which change sunlight into electricity.

solution A uniform mixture formed when one substance is completely dissolved in another substance.

sonar A means of detecting objects underwater through the use of sound waves.

species A group of similar organisms that are able to produce fertile offspring together.

spinneret A tube at the rear end of a spider that produces silk in the form of a thread, used to spin webs.

storm surge Water that is pushed toward the shore by strong winds, often caused by hurricanes as they move near land.

supernova The brilliant light and energy resulting from the explosion of a star at the end of its life.

suspension bridge A bridge whose roadway is suspended from cables attached to large towers at both ends.

T

tallow Solid animal fat that is sometimes used in the making of candles and soap.

tapetum A layer of cells in the back of the eye that reflects light, making it easier for certain animals to see in dim light.

tetanus An infectious bacterial disease that causes muscle spasms.

thermostat A device that controls the temperature in a room or an entire house.

threatened Likely to become endangered in the future.

toxin A poisonous substance produced by plants, animals, and bacteria.

U

ultraviolet Producing wavelengths that are shorter than visible light but longer than X-rays.

USB An interface that allows a computer to connect to another device, such as a keyboard. *USB* stands for *universal serial bus*.

V

vaccine A medicine, made of dead or weakened germs, that trains a person's body to fight that germ.

vapor 1. A gas.

2. Tiny but visible particles that float in the air, such as smoke or steam.

vertebra A segment of the backbone. The plural of *vertebra* is *vertebrae*.

virus 1. A tiny particle that can cause different types of illnesses by entering a person's body through the nose, the mouth, or breaks in the skin.

2. A computer program that is usually hidden within another program. It copies itself and spreads throughout the computer, causing damage.

W

wind turbine A machine that turns the power of the wind into electrical energy.

X

xylem The woody stem of a plant, which carries water to the leaves.

Index

Illustrations are indicated by **boldface**. When they fall within a page span, the entire span is **boldface**.

Photo credits

KEY: TtB - Top to bottom; BG - Background; CL - Clockwise from top left; LtR - Left to right

SS - Shutterstock; GY - Getty; AL - Alamy Stock Photo

Illustrations by Felipe Galindo on pages: Back cover, 2, 18-19, 37, 40-41, 47, 52-53, 56-57, 80-81, 82-83, 86-87, 92-93, 96, 98-99, 102-103, 104-105, 132-133, 141, 157, 158-159, 171

Illustrations by Ken Krug on pages: Back cover, 54-55, 62-63, 64, 70-71, 89, 90-91, 94-95, 106-107, 136, 146, 148-149, 168-169, 173, 180-181

FRONT COVER BG: ©KannaA/SS

BACK COVER BG: ©KannaA/SS, TtB: ©mbolina/GY, ©Johnny Dao/AL, ©Pete Saloutos/GY, ©Gang Liu/AL, ©Olga Besnard/SS

p. 1: ©KannaA/SS; p. 2 TtB: ©Viktord50/GY, ©Odoroaga Monica/AL, ©Hero Images Inc./AL, ©iStock.com, ©ChrisGorgio/GY; p. 4: ©Michael Lee/GY; p. 5: See credit information for pp. 34-35; pp. 6-7 BG: ©Catmando/SS, p. 6 CL: ©Bierchen/SS, ©Andrejs Pidjass/SS, ©Vishnevskiy Vasily/SS, p. 7 TtB: ©Joe Ferrer/AL, ©Arjo Van Timmerman/EyeEm/GY, ©Matt_Gibson/GY, ©Donald M. Jones/Minden Pictures/GY; pp. 8-9 BG: ©grafovi/GY, p. 8: ©Sabena Jane Blackbird/AL, p. 9 CL: ©TOM MCHUGH/GY, ©Swindaman/GY, ©Chris Mattison/AL, ©Visuals Unlimited, Inc./Joe McDonald/GY; pp. 10-11 BG: ©Nastya Pirieva/SS, CL: ©Nastya Pirieva/SS, ©Nastya Pirieva/SS, p. 11: ©Mike Parry/Minden Pictures/GY; pp. 12-13 BG: ©Panoramic Images/GY, ©agoxa/SS, p. 13 TtB: ©Jacek Jasinski/SS, ©reptiles4all/GY, ©Henrik Larsson/SS, ©Chris Minihane/GY; pp. 14-15 BG: ©Dante Fenolio/GY, Bottom LtR: ©Stuart Westmorland/GY, ©Nature Picture Library/AL, ©Solvin Zankl/AL, ©Widder/HBOI/GY, p. 15 TtB: ©James R.D. Scott/GY, ©bjonesmedia/GY; pp. 16-17 BG: ©Ryan M. Bolton/SS, p. 16: ©EcoPrint/SS, p. 17 CL: ©Vitaly Titov & Maria Sidelnikova/SS, ©NatalieJean/SS, ©Paulo Oliveira/AL, ©Ilya D. Gridnev/SS; pp. 18-19 BG: ©Viktord50/GY, p. 19: ©Photo of Steven Kutcher by Harry Chamberlain, courtesy of Steven Kutcher, http://home.earthlink.net/~skutcher/; pp. 20-21 BG: ©Design Pics Inc/AL, p. 21 CL: ©Suzi Eszterhas/Minden Pictures/GY, ©Alan Vernon/GY, ©Cameron Rutt/GY; pp. 22-23 BG: ©Ondrej Prosicky/SS, Bottom LtR: By ©Karta24 [FAL or CC BY-SA 4.0-3.0-2.5-2.0-1.0 (http://creativecommons.org/licenses/by-sa/4.0-3.0-2.5-2.0-1.0)], via Wikimedia Commons, ©Tim Zurowski/GY, ©KellyNelson/SS, ©Anthony Mercieca/Science Source, p. 23: ©WIKI Commons, ©DEA PICTURE LIBRARY/GY, ©mbolina/GY; pp. 24-25 BG: ©Mark Carwardine/Minden Pictures/GY, ©Bottom LtR: ©blickwinkel/AL, ©all images copyright of Jamie Lamb - elusive - images.co.uk/GY, ©Sicha69/GY; pp. 26-27 BG: ©Don Johnston_IH/ALp, Bottom LtR: ©Perry Correll/SS, ©chameleonseye/GY, ©CathyKeifer/GY, ©Thomas Kitchin & Victoria Hurst/Design Pics/GY, ©DougLemke/GY, ©Liliboas/GY, p. 27: ©jack0m/GY; pp. 28-29 BG: ©Supserstock, p. 29 CL: ©Visuals Unlimited, Inc./Thomas Marent/GY, ©mazzzur/GY, ©Cyril Ruoso/Minden Pictures/GY, ©USO/GY; pp. 30-31 BG: ©Katsumi Murouchi/GY, CL: ©FatCamera/GY, ©LWA/GY, ©tatyana_aleksieva/GY, ©LWA/GY, ©Shalom Ormsby/GY, ©Jupiterimages/GY, ©RooM the Agency/AL; pp. 32-33 BG: ©Image Source/AL, LtR: ©Sergei Fadeichev/GY, ©IPGGutenbergUKLtd/GY, ©Juergen Schwarz/Stringer/GY, ©imageBROKER/AL, ©PA Images/AL, ©dpa picture alliance archive/AL; pp. 34-35 BG: ©Monkey Business Images/SS, CL: ©Al Tielemans/Sports Illustrated, ©Al Tielemans/Sports Illustrated, ©Al Tielemans/Sports Illustrated, ©ASSOCIATED PRESS, ©Al Tielemans/Sports Illustrated, ©Al Tielemans/Sports Illustrated; pp. 36-37 BG: ©Baronb/SS, p. 36: ©Robert Cianflone/GY; pp. 38-39 BG: ©Ryan McVay/GY, p. 38: ©andriocolt/GY, p. 39: ©Erik Isakson/GY, ©Cappi Thompson/GY; pp. 40-41 BG: ©Maxim Tupikov/SS, ©Olga Besnard, p. 41 TtB: ©Alexander Demianchuk/GY, ©TOM MIHALEK/GY, ©Sergei Fadeichev/GY, ©Ryan McVay/GY; pp. 42-43 BG: ©ithinksky/GY, Bottom LtR: ©Pete Saloutos/GY, ©Peter Dazeley/GY, ©Portland Press Herald/GY, ©Dave King/GY, p. 43 TtB: ©Dave Reede/GY, ©James Ferrie/EyeEm/GY, ©Image Source/GY; pp. 44-45 BG: ©Hans Bezard/Agence Zoom/GY, p. 45 CL: ©Myles Cummings/EyeEm/GY, ©gbh007/GY, ©Idea Images/AL, ©Sean Prior/AL; pp. 46-47 BG: ©Andrey Yurlov/SS, ©steamroller_blues/SS; pp. 48-49 Time lapse images: ©John W. McDonough, p. 49: ©ASSOCIATED PRESS; pp. 50-51 BG: ©Katsumi Murouchi/GY, CL: ©Stephen Wilkes/GY, ©Dorothy Alexander/AL, ©Sharon West/AL, ©Sergey Novikov/AL, ©Dodge/GY, ©Stephen Wilkes/GY, ©Betty LaRue/AL, ©dnaveh/AL, ©bdspn/GY; pp. 52-53 BG: ©Ricardo Liberato/GY, ©DEA/G. DAGLI ORTI/GY, p. 53: ©Marcos Carvalho/SS, ©Raj Krish/SS; pp. 54-55 BG: ©JTB Photo/GY; pp. 56-57 BG: ©B. Franklin/SS, CL: ©Stan Shebs/Creative Commons, ©Thomas Marine, Library of Congress, ©ASSOCIATED PRESS; pp. 58-59 BG: ©Jody Dingle/SS, LtR: ©All historic photos courtesy of National Park Service, U.S. Department of the Interior; pp. 60-61 BG: ©Sebastian Kopp/EyeEm/GY, pp. 60-61CL: ©Michael Doolittle/AL, ©Michael Doolittle/AL, ©Michael Doolittle/AL, ©Mathias Beinling/AL, ©Michael Doolittle/AL, ©Michael Doolittle/AL, ©Michael Doolittle/AL; pp. 62-63 BG: ©Katsumi Murouchi/GY, p. 62: ©simoly/SS; pp. 64-65 BG: ©SafakOguz/GY, p. 64 LtR: ©Johnny Dao/AL, ©NASA Photo/AL, p. 65 CL: ©Bloomberg/GY, ©Bloomberg/GY, ©Oregon State University, ©John B. Carnett/GY; pp. 66-67 BG: ©AL-Travelpicture/GY, Bottom LtR: ©Mike Hill/GY, ©Mickrick/GY, ©Steve Estvanik/SS, ©elmvilla/GY, ©Pete Ryan/GY, ©Kyle W. Anstey/GY, ©DurkTalsma/GY, ©by wildestanimal/GY; pp. 68-69 BG: ©Louie Psihoyos/GY, CL: ©John Elk III/AL, ©Curtis Slepian, ©Curtis Slepian, ©Curtis Slepian, ©David McNew/GY; pp. 70-71 BG: ©Kathy Von Torne/GY, ©John Elk/GY, p. 71 TtB: ©Willard/GY, ©Josef Mohyla/GY, ©PhotoTalk/GY, ©Australian Scenics/GY; pp. 72-73 BG: ©BEST-PHOTOS/GY, CL: ©Izel Photography/AL, ©Craig Auckland/ArcaidImages/GY, ©StellaPhotography/AL, ©B Christopher/AL, ©maxstock2/AL, ©Liquid Light/AL; pp. 74-75 BG: ©Chris Graythen/GY, Top LtR: ©Joe Raedle/GY, ©Chris Graythen/GY, ©Cheryl Casey/SS, Bottom LtR: ©Handout/GY, ©MIGUEL ROJO/GY, ©Fairfax Media/GY, ©Michelly Rall/GY; pp. 76-77 BG: ©dem10/GY, p. 76: ©technotr/GY, p. 77 LtR: ©Universal Images Group North America LLC/AL, ©milena moiola/Alamy; pp. 78-79 BG: ©Katsumi Murouchi/GY, CL: ©Panther Media GmbH/AL, ©Gang Liu/AL, ©Hero Images/GY, ©Garry McMichael/GY, ©steinphoto/GY; pp. 80-81 BG: ©Kemter/GY, CL: ©Bill Pugliano/GY, ©Anton Gvozdikov/AL ©Odoroaga Monica/AL; pp. 82-83 BG: ©View Stock/AL, Bottom LtR: ©Sergiy Serdyuk/AL, ©Maglev photos courtesy of Transrapid USA, Top 5 LtR: ©Shanghai Maglev photo by Lee Prince, ©ValeStock/GY, ©holgs/GY; pp. 84-85 BG: ©Karsten Bidstrup/GY, p. 84: ©ilbusca/GY; pp. 86-87 BG: ©P A Thompson/GY, LtR: ©evan66/SS, ©Handout/GY; pp. 88-89 BG: ©Education Images/GY; CL: ©Mickrick/GY, ©Simon Brooke-Webb/AL; pp. 90-91 BG: ©Katsumi Murouchi/GY, ©NASA, ©NASA Photo by Jim Ross, ©NASA; pp. 92-93 BG: ©matdesign24/GY, ©Daniel Borzynski/AL, p. 93 TtB: ©Einar Muoni/SS, ©Hadrian/SS; pp. 94-95 BG: ©Vera Volkova/SS; pp. 96-97 BG: ©Natali Glado/SS; p. 97 CL: ©Bruce Rolff/SS, ©Vadym Andrushchenko/SS, ©Creative Commons; pp. 98-99 BG: ©sorendls/GY, CL: ©Science & Society Picture Library/GY, ©Maudib/GY, ©Popperfoto/GY; pp. 100-101 BG: ©Caro Sheridan/Splityarn/GY; Zipper: ©Scott Weichert/GY, ©ZUMA Press, Inc./AL, p. 101 TtB: ©Torsten Dietrich/SS, ©curtoicurto/GY, ©By NASA (National Aeronautics and Space Administration) [Public domain], via Wikimedia Commons; pp. 102-103 BG: ©xxmmxx/GY, p. 103 TtB: ©H. Mark Weidman Photography/AL, ©Vicki Beaver/AL, NASA; pp. 104-105 BG: ©Katsumi Murouchi/GY, p. 105 TtB: ©Photo 12/AL, ©maxmihai/GY, ©Stanisic Vladimir/SS; pp. 106-107 BG: ©Sam Diephuis/GY, p. 106: ©ZCHE/FEND (Supplied by WENN)/Newscom, p. 107: ©Xinhua/AL, ©ASSOCIATED PRESS; pp. 108-109 BG: ©Geography Photos/GY, CL: ©Design Pics Inc/GY, ©Lev Dolgachov/AL , ©RyanKing999/GY, ©Steele/GY, ©George Rose/GY, Bottom LtR: ©Zoonar GmbH/AL, ©scanrail/GY; pp. 110-111 BG: ©johnpaulramirez/GY, CL: ©valdis torms/SS, ©AFP/GY, ©Geri Lavrov/GY, ©chert61/GY, ©Norman Chan, ©Norman Chan, ©Greg da Silva/SS; pp. 112-113 BG: ©Steven Xiong/EyeEm/GY, CL: ©Amnajtandee/GY, ©Balefire/SS, ©Rischgitz/GY, ©R studio T; Elnur/SS, ©Todd Davidson/GY, p. 113: ©Panther Media GmbH/AL; pp. 114-115 BG: ©pinglabel/GY, ©Encyclopedia Britannica/UIG/GY, p. 115: ©PC Plus Magazine/GY; pp. 116-117 BG: ©MirageC/GY, LtR: ©adventtr/GY, ©AlessandroZocc/GY, ©Bloomberg/GY, ©ET-ARTWORKS/iStock/GY, ©Bloomberg/GY, VCG/GY, ©B Christopher/AL; pp. 118-119 BG: ©Katsumi Murouchi/GY, CL: ©theodore liasi/AL, Emma Gibbs/GY, ©Hero Images Inc./AL, ©Amnajtandee/GY, ©Randy Duchaine/AL, ©WHITE HOUSE POOL (ISP POOL IMAGES)/GY, ©shock/AL; pp. 120-121 BG: ©iStock.com, p. 121: ©BSIP SA/AL; pp. 122-123 BG: ©Mack7777/SS, CL: ©NASA, ©NASA, ©NASA, ©Micahel Doolittle/AL, ©NASA, ©NASA; pp. 124-125 BG: ©NASA and the Night Sky Network, ©NASA/JPL-Caltech/Harvard-Smithsonian CfA; pp. 126-127 BG: ©NASA, CL: ©NASA/JPL-Caltech/SwRI/MSSS/Betsy Asher Hall/Gervasio Robles, ©NASA, ©By NASA/JPL/DLR [Public domain], via Wikimedia Commons, ©NASA, ©NASA; pp. 128-129 BG: ©NASA/JPL-Caltech, CL: ©ESA/ATG medialab; ©background: ESO/S. Brunier, ©Science History Images/AL, ©Science History Images/AL, ©NASA/JPL-Caltech, ©NASA/JPL-Caltech, p. 129 TtB: ©NASA, ©NASA; pp. 130-131 BG: ©Richard Wainscoat/AL, CL: ©Marusa Bradac/Hubble Space Telescope/W. M. Keck Observatory, ©NASA/JPL-Caltech, ©W. M. KECK OBSERVATORY, ©W. M. KECK OBSERVATORY; pp. 132-133 BG: ©Katsumi Murouchi/GY, p. 133: ©NASA, ©NASA/ Bill Stafford; pp. 134-135 BG: ©Lane Oatey/Blue Jean Images/GY, CL: ©Gleb Semenjuk/SS, ©JUAN GAERTNER/SCIENCE PHOTO LIBRARY/GY, ©By NIAID/NIH (NIAID Flickr's photostream) [Public domain], via Wikimedia Commons, ©Sebastian Kaulitzki/AL, ©Blacqbook/SS; pp. 136-137 BG: ©BWFolsom/GY, p. 137 TtB: ©forgiss/GY, ©Arnold Media/GY, ©BSIP SA/AL, ©MedStockPhotos/AL, ©LH Images/AL; pp. 138-139 BG: ©Pixtum/GY, LtR: ©Sebastian Kaulitzki/SS, ©fstop123/GY, ©voylodyon/SS, ©Dmitry Lobanov/SS, p. 139: ©Davies/GY; pp. 140-141 BG: ©magicmine/GY, LtR: ©new wave/SS, ©3D Clinic/GY, ©Roger Harris/SPL/GY, ©ChrisGorgio/GY; pp. 142-143 BG: ©Ed Reschke/GY, ©LEONELLO CALVETTI/GY, ©BSIP/UIG/GY, p. 143 TtB: ©John Giustina/GY, ©Jonathan Kim/GY; pp. 144-145 BG: ©stilllifephotographer/GY, p. 144: ©Spotmatik/GY, p. 145: ©Dorling Kindersley/GY; pp. 146-147 BG: ©Media for Medical/GY, p. 146: ©Photography by Paula Thomas/GY, p. 147 CL: ©andresr/GY, ©Sueddeutsche Zeitung Photo/AL, ©E+/GY, ©RichLegg/iStock/GY, ©Blend Images/AL; pp. 148-149 BG: ©Katsumi Murouchi/GY, p. 149 CL: ©Tim Graham/GY, ©The Washington Post/GY, ©Boston Globe/GY; pp. 150-151 BG: ©Aeriform/GY, p. 150 TtB: ©John Lund/GY, ©NASA/JPL, p. 151: ©Courtesy of Time For Kids; pp. 152-153 BG: ©mlharing/GY, p. 152 TtB: ©By Yellowstone National Park from Yellowstone NP, USA (Wolf leaving shipping container in Rose Creek pen) [CC BY 2.0 (http://creativecommons.org/licenses/by/2.0) or Public domain], via Wikimedia Commons, ©georgesanker.com/AL, p. 153 CL: ©Ingo Arndt/Minden Pictures/GY, ©By Yellowstone National Park from Yellowstone NP, USA (Beaver) [Public domain], via Wikimedia Commons, ©Danita Delimont/AL, ©BirdImages/GY, ©JREden/GY, ©Mark Miller Photos/GY, ©Bryant Aardema/AL; pp. 154-155 BG: ©mapichai/GY, ©De Agostini Picture Library/GY, ©TefiM/GY, p. 155 TtB: ©ttsz/GY, ©Fir Mamat/AL; pp. 156-157 BG: ©Christopher Furlong/GY, p. 157: ©dpa picture alliance archive/AL; pp. 158-159 BG: ©Dougal Waters/GY, p. 94: ©Putu Sayoga/GY, p. 95 TtB: ©laremenko/ GY, ©Chris Pearsall/AL; pp. 160-161 BG: ©baranozdemir/GY, CL: ©Jyrki Komulainen/GY, ©Sean Gallup/GY, ©AFP/GY, ©Lya_Cattel/GY, ©Sean Gallup/GY; pp. 162-163 BG: ©Anna_Om/GY, Papers: ©Robbi/SS, Richard Ellis/AL; pp. 164-165 BG: ©PJF Military Collection/AL, LtR: ©RosalreneBetancourt 5/AL, ©BIOSPHOTO/AL, ©NOAA, p. 165: ©Kip Evans/AL; pp. 166-167 BG: ©Katsumi Murouchi/GY, Steps 1-7: ©JeffG/AL, ©Minerva Studio/AL, ©David S. Holloway/GY, ©Jeff Greenberg 6 of 6/AL, ©Education Images/GY, ©Richard Levine/AL, ©Torontonian/AL, p. 167: ©Portland Press Herald/GY; pp. 168-169 BG: ©Stefano Politi Markovina/AL; pp. 170-171 BG: ©Michael Lee/GY, Steps 1-5: ©New York Daily News/GY, ©Spencer Platt/GY, ©Guy Calaf/Polaris, ©Altrendo Travel/GY, ©Young Yun/GY; pp. 172-173 BG: ©Werner Dieterich/GY, p. 172 TtB: ©Children's Discovery Museum of San Jose, ©Photo by Michelle Frehsee, Courtesy of Brattleboro Museum & Art Center; pp. 174-175 BG: ©Oliver Furrer/GY, Bottom LtR: ©Model Images/AL, Zia Soleil/GY, ©3sbworld/GY; pp. 176-177 BG: ©mahout/SS, Steps 1-6: ©Margie Hurwich/SS, ©Stacie Stauff Smith Photography/SS, ©Joy Fera/SS, ©Fera/SS, ©Sylvie Bouchard/SS, p. 177 TtB: ©age fotostock/AL, ©Rachel Grazias/SS; pp. 178-179 BG: ©Peter Dazeley/GY, p. 178 TtB: ©John Lund/GY, ©Jeff Greenberg/GY, ©Radius Images/AL, ©Hero Images/GY, ©Bob Caddick/AL,©Bob Caddick/AL, p. 179 CL: ©Elnur Amikishiyev/AL, ©PA Images/AL, ©Bill Rome/GY, ©Mark Fagelson/AL; pp. 180-181 BG: ©Katsumi Murouchi/GY, p. 180 TtB: ©EuToch/GY, ©9george/GY, ©Kansas City Star/GY, ©Aradan/GY, ©Aradan/GY; p. 185: ©mapichai/GY

TOP 5 Sources
Page 55: Aalto University, Finland, bridge. *aalto.fi/en/longspan.html* Page 61: World Atlas, *worldatlas.com/articles/10-tallest-buildings-in-the-world.html* Page 156 American Wind Energy Association, *awea.org/state-fact-sheets* Page 177 Roller Coaster DataBase, *rcdb.com* Page 178 Bruner, Raisa, "The 10 Most Viral Videos of 2016." *TIME*, December 10, 2016. Accessed at *time.com.*